RAND

Evaluating Agency Alternative Dispute Resolution Programs

A Users' Guide to Data Collection and Use

Elizabeth Rolph, Erik Moller

Prepared for the
Administrative Conference of the United States

The Institute for Civil Justice

The mission of the Institute for Civil Justice is to help make the civil justice system more efficient and more equitable by supplying policymakers and the public with the results of objective, empirically based, analytic research. The ICJ facilitates change in the civil justice system by analyzing trends and outcomes, identifying and evaluating policy options, and bringing together representatives of different interests to debate alternative solutions to policy problems. The Institute builds on a long tradition of RAND research characterized by an interdisciplinary, empirical approach to public policy issues and rigorous standards of quality, objectivity, and independence.

ICJ research is supported by pooled grants from corporations, trade and professional associations, and individuals; by government grants and contracts; and by private foundations. The Institute disseminates its work widely to the legal, business, and research communities, and to the general public. In accordance with RAND policy, all Institute research products are subject to peer review before publication. ICJ publications do not necessarily reflect the opinions or policies of the research sponsors or of the ICJ Board of Overseers.

Board of Overseers

Preface

The mission of the Institute for Civil Justice is to help make the civil justice system more efficient and more equitable by providing policymakers and the public with the results of objective research. Consistent with this mission, the Institute occasionally provides special assistance to public agencies in the civil justice system concerned with the system's performance.

This document was produced at the request of the Administrative Conference of the United States, which asked the Institute for Civil Justice to prepare a manual and develop prototype data-collection instruments to assist those with responsibility for evaluating federal agency alternative dispute resolution programs. The manual discusses issues in designing evaluations, lays out approaches to data collection, provides sample data analysis plans, and includes a number of prototype data-collection instruments.

For information about the Institute for Civil Justice, contact

Dr. Deborah R. Hensler
Director, Institute for Civil Justice
RAND
1700 Main Street, P.O. Box 2138
Santa Monica, CA 90407-2138
(310) 393-0411, ext. 7803
Internet: Deborah_Hensler@rand.org

A profile of the ICJ, abstracts of its publications, and ordering information can also be found on RAND's home page on the World Wide Web at **http://www.rand.org/** and on RAND's gopher server at **info.rand.org.**

Contents

viii

Tables

Acknowledgments

We wish to acknowledge the financial assistance of the Administrative Conference of the United States, without which this research would not be possible. We additionally acknowledge the assistance of Nancy Miller and Maryann Gray for their comments on earlier drafts of this report. Last, we are indebted to Julie Brown for her assistance in creating the survey instruments, Phyllis Gilmore for her editorial assistance, and Pat Williams for her secretarial support.

1. Introduction

This manual is intended to assist those undertaking or simply contemplating evaluations of federal agency alternative dispute resolution (ADR) programs.[1] Our goals are to clarify the reasons evaluations are conducted, provide an overview of the major evaluation design issues, describe the process of data instrument design, present a few sample analysis plans, and provide a set of prototype data-collection instruments that may be tailored to suit many agency evaluation needs. This manual is *not* intended to be a comprehensive treatment of evaluation design and conduct; users should consult the extensive evaluation literature and obtain statistical support at *all* stages of the evaluation.

Why Should Program Evaluations Be Conducted?

Goal-oriented evaluations are conducted to answer two fundamental questions about program effectiveness:[2]

- **Is the program accomplishing the goals we have set for it?**
- **How can we improve the program's performance?**

Evaluations may be conducted to demonstrate the program's effectiveness to an outside audience or simply to identify ways to improve the effectiveness of the program.

Goals

Programs are designed and put in place to accomplish certain goals. Sometimes these goals are clearly specified; more often they are less clear or even in conflict. Furthermore, it is entirely possible that program goals will change over time. The purpose of an evaluation usually is to determine whether or not, or the degree to which, a program is achieving each of its current underlying goals.

---

[1]Support for the development of this manual and the prototype data-collection instruments was provided by the Administrative Conference of the United States and the Institute for Civil Justice/RAND.

[2]This manual concentrates on goal-oriented evaluations. For a brief description of various other kinds of evaluations, see Herman et al. (1989).

Improved Performance

Programs often depend on unique designs and function in unique contexts. Therefore, contextual and implementation factors may have a substantial bearing on program outcomes. Learning something about the nature and role of these factors in the performance of a program may give evaluators insights into how a program can be modified to improve performance along important dimensions.

When Should Evaluations Be Conducted?

Consideration of *when* to conduct evaluations depends on two very important issues: *program maturity* and *baseline data*.

Goal-oriented evaluations should be sensitive to the maturity of the program under scrutiny. Programs typically go through an unsettled early-implementation phase, and outcomes that are measured during this phase are likely to be different from those of the mature program. To learn about its long-term potential, a program must be evaluated in its mature state. Evaluators must judge the maturity of a given program.

However, evaluations usually depend on some point of comparison: Is this program better than the old way of doing the job, or is it better than an alternative program? To have a point of comparison, it may be necessary to collect baseline data on outcomes of interest before the program has been implemented.[3] Therefore, it is important that evaluation planning begin *before* the program is implemented; if necessary, baseline data for the evaluation should be collected at this point, as well.

---

[3]See the discussion of study design below.

2. An Overview of Evaluation Design Issues

A number of items are key to conducting a successful evaluation. This section identifies and briefly highlights the main issues, but we urge evaluators to read widely and obtain additional expertise in each of these areas. The main issues are

- **Identifying program goals**[1]
- **Developing appropriate measures of outcomes**
- **Collecting the right type of data for the measures**
- **Choosing a study design**
- **Developing an analysis plan.**

Program Goals

The first step in any evaluation is to identify the program's goals. As we noted above, these goals may be murky; they may conflict with each other; and/or they may change over time. But the evaluation must resolve the murkiness; make appropriate choices, if necessary, among goals that may have changed; and note inconsistencies among goals. In short, the evaluator must be absolutely clear about the characteristics that are being used to assess the program. Without a clear and defensible specification of the goals, evaluators cannot make appropriate choices regarding study design, and they cannot draw useful conclusions from the study about the performance and ultimate value of the program.

---

[1]The evaluation literature often refers to goals and objectives separately and as distinct concepts. When they are discussed separately, the term *goals* usually refers to the broad, long-term benefits the program is intended to have, while the term *objectives* refers to the concrete intermediate targets set up as steps to the longer-term goals. When the goals of the program being evaluated are especially complex and/or difficult to measure, it is very important to clearly specify measurable objectives that will serve as defensible proxies for progress toward these long-term goals. In the case of new ADR programs, the goals are likely to be reasonably straightforward and measurable; therefore, in this manual, we do not generally distinguish between goals and objectives. Rather, we simply refer to program goals.

Appropriate Measures

To guide data collection, research questions should be developed on several aspects of the program, including

- **Important program outcomes**
- **Participant and case characteristics**
- **Program implementation characteristics.**

Once program goals have been identified, the next step is to develop a more specific set of researchable questions and outcome measures that speak to the program goals. For example, if one of the program goals is to reduce costs, the elements of the costs that should be reduced must be identified and defined.[2] Whose costs—the agency's, the disputant's? What costs—attorneys' fees, witness costs, administrative costs?

If an evaluation is to have interpretive power—that is, the ability to go beyond a bare assessment of program outcomes to explaining the outcomes and offering suggestions for program improvement—it must include additional information on those case and program implementation characteristics that are likely to influence the outcomes of interest. For example, if a program fails to achieve its goals, we cannot know whether the failure stemmed from a weakness in the design of the new program or from some failure to implement it effectively. Case characteristics should include information on the nature of the dispute, its complexity, and attributes of the disputants. Program implementation characteristics might include such factors as eligibility rules, staff training, and/or education and outreach.

The purpose of the evaluation, the evaluation goals, the evaluation budget, and the availability of data and technical expertise will combine to determine the thoroughness of any evaluation, but even a limited effort can be very useful. For example, even if constraints dictate a very limited effort, it is usually possible to gather basic information on the key outcomes of cost, time to disposition, and agency satisfaction, as well as information on the characteristics of each dispute. If collected in a properly designed study, even these data can yield very useful results about the effectiveness of the program. Of course, a more comprehensive data-collection effort, one, for example, that solicits responses from disputants on

---

[2]For a comprehensive list of outcomes that are relevant to the measurement of program goals, see Administrative Conference of the United States (1993).

their reactions and from agency personnel on implementation characteristics, will permit a much more thorough evaluation.

Types of Approaches

Methods and data are often described as being

- **Quantitative** or
- **Qualitative.**

Which type of approach is most appropriate for an evaluation will depend on what information is available to the evaluator and on what type is most useful for answering the particular questions at issue. Evaluations often include both types of data, sometimes independently to address different questions in the same study and sometimes in tandem to add strength to particular conclusions.

Quantitative Methods

Quantitative methods are the methods most frequently used in evaluation studies. These methods are generally used to measure prespecified, quantifiable program effects. They entail measuring, summarizing, and comparing and should, when possible, be coupled with an experimental study design with a control or comparison group (see below). Typical sources of quantitative data include abstracted records and standardized survey instruments.

Like all methods, quantitative methods offer some strengths and some weaknesses. Without question, they allow objective comparisons of performance outcomes, and this is likely to be the goal of an evaluation of an agency ADR program. Such methods also can be less expensive than a purely qualitative study. However, to draw valid conclusions using quantitative methods, the study population must be of ample size; the available data must be of high enough quality to support a statistical analysis; and the general nature of the relationships between the quantities being measured should be understood "going in." Furthermore, these methods are not designed to uncover the subtleties of program implementation and participant reactions, and often they are unable to provide persuasive causal links between program design features and important outcome measures.[3]

---

[3]See Patton (1987), pp. 8–11.

6

Because sometimes the requirements of a quantitative study seem somewhat daunting, let us note that most studies of court-annexed ADR programs have successfully employed these methods.

Qualitative Methods

Qualitative methods can also be used in evaluations. These methods yield data on the behavior and perceptions of participants in the process. They are particularly useful for gathering information regarding the internal dynamics of the program (identifying bottlenecks and points of particular effectiveness), identifying unintended program consequences, and gaining insights into possible causal links between program design, implementation, and outcomes. Qualitative methods are also useful when the study population is too small or diffuse to permit the use of quantitative methods.[4]

The usual sources of qualitative data include observation, individual interviews, focus groups, and written documents. Interviewing may provide somewhat more information and may offer the opportunity to probe for sensitive information from individual respondents.[5] Focus groups offer the opportunity for participant interaction and consensus formation. Therefore, conclusions may be more broadly applicable.[6] While data-collection instruments for quantitative studies are highly structured, instruments or guides for qualitative studies are usually open-ended and suggestive. The quality of qualitative data is extremely dependent on the skill of those collecting it.

The price of gathering richer and more detailed information on a smaller number of cases that frequently are *not* randomly selected is losing the ability to generalize beyond the specific population being observed or queried. Thus, the conclusions of qualitative studies are likely to be less defensible than those presented in quantitative studies.[7]

Evaluation Designs

An evaluation design is, in essence, a study plan that determines who will be exposed to the new program and how the results of exposure and nonexposure

---

[4]See Patton (1987) for a good discussion of the use of qualitative methods in evaluation. See also Rossi (1979).

[5]See Fowler (1984) for a discussion of interview survey research methods. See also Patton (1987).

[6]See Krueger (1988) regarding focus group methodology.

[7]See Patton (1987), pp. 8–11; Fowler (1984), pp. 64–68.

one or more programs. It typically entails a comparison either among several program options or between the new program and the status quo. If comparisons are to reflect *only* the effects of the different programs, or "treatments," then the populations of subjects and their experiences should be identical except for the program. That is, *everything else* in the environment must be held constant.[8] There are several possible study designs; some achieve this ideal better than others. They include use of

- **a true control group**
- **a nonequivalent control group**
- **a before and after design.**

Within each of these designs, the evaluator will need to address sampling issues. In the simplest situation, the study sample will consist of the entire population, so no sampling need be done. More commonly, budget and other practical constraints will limit the size of the study sample. Two principles should be observed when making sampling decisions: (1) whenever possible use randomization to select the sample rather than a sample of convenience, and (2) all else being equal, the larger the sample, the better. Discussing the details of actual sampling plans is beyond the scope of this guide.[9]

True Control Group

If the evaluation is to provide information on the effects of the program, it must (1) ensure the population in the ADR program is like that in the control (or status quo) group, and (2) hold all else constant. That is, the evaluation must use an experimental design. In an experimental design, cases are each *randomly assigned* to the dispute resolution environments that are being compared. These environments must both be operating contemporaneously; the traditional dispute resolution mechanism and the new ADR program both must be running smoothly and be available to receive randomly assigned disputes. *This is the gold standard of evaluation designs.*

---

[8]For example, if one simply measures "time to disposition" for cases in a new agency ADR program, compares that time with the "time to disposition" for cases handled before the program was adopted, and discovers the time to be shorter, one *cannot* conclude that the ADR program caused the reduction. Perhaps the disputes in the new caseload are, on average, of a less contentious nature or perhaps those cases that the new program captures are the less contentious disputes. A well-designed evaluation will gather additional information that can reduce or eliminate alternative explanations for observed outcomes.

[9]See Kalton (1983) for a good elementary treatment of sampling.

An evaluation based on a true control group design should include the following steps:

1. Identify the population (the disputes) eligible for the program under study to construct a sampling frame.

2. *Randomly* assign the disputes filed over some period of time to the new ADR program or to the old dispute process.

3. Gather information from both groups on characteristics that might affect their performance. This information should be useful in analyzing the similarity of the groups and adjusting for differences.

4. Measure the outcomes and dispute characteristics of interest for both groups in a standardized way.

In many situations, it may be impossible to assign cases randomly to the two programs or to obtain sufficient cases to draw statistically valid conclusions once they are divided between alternative treatments. Nonetheless, the possibility of using a design with a true control group should *always* be explored, because it provides the most statistically defensible results. Evaluators of agency ADR programs should also be aware that courts frequently use randomized control groups when evaluating their court-annexed ADR and other reform programs. Randomization is not necessarily a legal, constitutional, or logistical problem in disputing environments.

Nonequivalent Control Group

Designs using "nonequivalent" control groups depend on comparisons of two similar groups, although subjects have not been randomly assigned to the two programs. Such similar groups may be the population of cases in two different agency offices that handle similar cases, for example, or cases handled by different agencies encountering similar matters. This design depends on the following steps:

1. Find similar populations of cases.

2. Gather information from both groups on characteristics that might affect their performance. This information should be useful in analyzing the similarity of the groups and adjusting for differences.

3. Measure the outcomes and dispute characteristics of interest for both groups in a standardized way.

Before and After Designs

The above designs attempt to set up little experiments; the results of two options are compared, holding everything else constant. If only the new program will be in place and available for study, comparisons should be made of *before and after* outcomes. Studies using single-group time series rely on identical data that are collected from the population of disputes at multiple points before, during, and after the implementation of the new program. This design requires the use of the same data-collection procedures and instruments, applied at standard points in the disputing process, and can give a reasonable picture of the program's effects on the outcomes measured.

A simple version of the single-group time series approach is the two-period Before and After design. With this design, identical information is collected before the new ADR program is implemented and after it has taken full effect. However, this design may only allow for informal comparisons. The data collected may not be comparable, since evaluations take substantial time, and during that time, important characteristics of the environment or the study population (the dispute mix, for example) may well have changed, quietly affecting the outcomes of interest. Unless it is clear that nothing important has changed over the time period in question, this design does not allow evaluators to distinguish between program effects and contextual effects. But it can be a relatively inexpensive, simple evaluation to mount, and therefore should be considered when resources and/or technical expertise are limited. While not the gold standard, Before and After studies can provide program administrators and policymakers with very useful insights and results.

Analysis Tools

If they are to yield answers to the evaluation questions, the data, once in hand, must be analyzed. Methods of analysis vary from simple descriptive tabulations to complex multivariate methods. If the evaluator is not familiar with even simple statistical methods, he or she should obtain the assistance of a statistician or policy analyst.

Descriptive Statistics

The most basic statistical tools give well-recognized numerical descriptions of the data. Typical tabulations include the frequencies of the different values of each variable being measured and other descriptive measures (means, medians, and variances). These measures can be compared for before and after periods around the implementation of ADR, for disputes assigned to ADR and non-ADR tracks within the office, and for other comparison groups of interest.

More Complex Statistical Methods

More complex analytical methods include cross tabulations and multiple regression. These multivariate methods can be used to test and describe relationships between the variables.

3. Developing a Data-Collection Plan

The discussion thus far has addressed general issues regarding the reasons for and issues associated with the conduct of an evaluation. Now, we turn specifically to the question of how to design a data-collection plan for an agency ADR program. There are five main steps in such a plan—several of which were discussed in Section 2:

- **Identifying program goals**
- **Developing appropriate measures**
- **Identifying appropriate data sources**
- **Developing data-collection instruments**
- **Collecting the data.**

Agency ADR Program Goals

The several and sometimes competing goals underlying the enactment of the Administrative Dispute Resolution Act, as well as the adoption or modification of most ADR programs, are to

- **Reduce costs**
- **Reduce delay**
- **Maintain or improve disputant satisfaction**
- **Preserve the equity of outcomes**
- **Promote a less contentious environment.**[1]

Comparison programs may be traditional dispute resolution mechanisms, other ADR programs, or previous versions of the same program.

The evaluation questions, then must be designed to address the following question: **Are These Goals Being Achieved?**

---

[1] Administrative Conference of the United States (1993) refers to these and other goals that may be relevant to an ADR program evaluation.

12

Research Questions and Measures

With these goals in mind, an evaluation rests on the following logical sequence:

TO BE SUCCESSFUL, AN ADR PROGRAM MUST

1. CAPTURE **and**

2. PERMANENTLY RESOLVE A SUBSTANTIAL PROPORTION OF

    1. THE ENTIRE TARGET CASELOAD **or**

    2. A PROBLEMATIC SUBPOPULATION OF THE CASELOAD

and

3. SHOW AN IMPROVEMENT IN OUTCOMES THAT REFLECT THE PROGRAM'S GOALS.

This logic gives rise to a set of research questions, associated measures, and ultimately an analysis plan. Table 1 presents a prototypical set of outcomes that speak to program goals and a corresponding set of measures or *performance indicators* that speak to the outcomes.[2] In addition, the list of outcomes accounts for case, disputant, and implementation characteristics, as identified in the above logical sequence, that are likely to affect the outcomes of importance.

Measures and Data Sources

Once the measures or performance indicators have been specified, the next step in designing the information collection component of an evaluation is to determine the best source of information for each of the measures and the best method for getting that information. Table 2 shows a matrix that can be used to link the measures developed for Table 1 to information sources and methods. We have filled in some of the cells, particularly when there is a link to the prototype survey instruments discussed in detail below and found in Appendices A through E. However, these links are only suggestive; appropriate choices depend very much on the evaluation context.

---

[2]These measures and the performance indicators are drawn from Administrative Conference of the United States (1993).

Table 1

Research Questions and Measures

What Proportion of Disputes Is Captured?
  Number of disputes in program

Are Disputes Successfully Resolved?
  Number of disputes settled before ADR
  Number of disputes settled in ADR
  Number of disputes settled before hearing
  Compliance with settlement agreement

Does the ADR Program Affect Outcomes That Reflect the Program's Goals?

  Does the ADR Program Affect the Equity of Dispute Resolution?
    Are disputes resolved differently between ADR and non-ADR
      procedures?
    Are disputants satisfied with the resolutions?

  Does the ADR Program Affect Time to Disposition?
    Time to disposition

  Does the ADR Program Affect Agency Costs (as administrator)?
    Administrative costs

  Does the ADR Program Affect Agency Costs (as disputant)?
    Agency disputant costs

  Does the ADR Program Affect Disputant Costs?
    Private disputant costs

  Does the ADR Program Affect Disputant Satisfaction?
    With procedure
    With neutral
    With outcome
    With implementation

  Does the ADR Program Affect Attorney Satisfaction?
    With procedure
    With neutral
    With outcome
    With implementation

  Does the ADR Program Affect Workplace Environment?
    Relationship between disputants
    Number of subsequent disputes
    Work environment
    Management attitudes

Are There Alternative Explanations for the Effects Observed?
  What are the Caseload Characteristics?
    Caseload characteristics

  Was the Program Effectively Implemented?
    Design
    Education/training of agency staff
    Education/training of disputants
    Resources
    Coordination

Table 2

Performance Indicators to Measuring Variables

Research Questions and Measures	Measuring Variables	Quantitative Sources[a]	Qualitative Sources[a]
What Proportion of Disputes Is Captured?			
Number of disputes in program	Number of disputes	Case abstraction form (aggregate statistic)	
Are Disputes Successfully Resolved?			
Number of disputes settled before ADR	Did dispute settle? When did dispute settle?	Disputant survey question 21 Attorney survey questions 8–14 Case abstraction form Sections C and D	
Number of disputes settled in ADR	Did dispute settle? When did dispute settle?	Disputant survey question 21 Attorney survey questions 8–14 Case abstraction form Sections C and D	
Number of disputes settled before hearing	Did dispute settle? When did dispute settle?	Disputant survey question 21 Attorney survey questions 8–14 Case abstraction form Sections C and D	
Compliance with settlement agreement	Have the disputants complied with the terms of the settlement agreement?	Case abstraction form Sections C and D	

Table 2—continued

Research Questions and Measures	Measuring Variables	Quantitative Sources[a]	Qualitative Sources[a]
Does the ADR Program Affect the Equity of Dispute Resolution?			
Are disputes resolved differently between ADR and non-ADR procedures?	Nature of outcome Amount of outcome	Disputant survey questions 17–20	
Are disputants satisfied with the resolution?	Disputant overall satisfaction with outcomes	Disputant survey questions 14–16	
Does the ADR Program Affect Time to Disposition?			
Time to disposition	Time of filing Time of disposition	Attorney survey questions 8–14 Case abstraction form Sections C and D	
Does the ADR Program Affect Agency Costs (as administrator)?			
Administrative costs	Program administrative costs Mediator costs Hearing officer costs	Evaluator survey question 3 Mediator survey questions 10–20	

Table 2—continued

Research Questions and Measures	Measuring Variables	Quantitative Sources[a]	Qualitative Sources[a]
Does the ADR Program Affect Agency Costs (as disputant)?			
Agency disputant costs	Costs of agency disputant time	Disputant survey questions 28–38	
	Attorneys' fees and costs	Attorney survey questions 20–31	
Does the ADR Program Affect Disputant Costs?			
Private disputant costs	Costs of private disputant time	Disputant survey questions 28–38	
	Attorneys' fees and costs	Attorney survey questions 20–31	
Does the ADR Program Affect Disputant Satisfaction?			
Disputant satisfaction with procedure	Disputant satisfaction with procedure measured along various dimensions including fairness, opportunity to be heard, control, and formality	Disputant survey questions 10d–10h and 11	
Disputant satisfaction with neutral	Disputant satisfaction with neutral based on competence, bias, and preparation	Disputant survey questions 12b–12g	
Disputant satisfaction with outcome	Disputant satisfaction with outcome	Disputant survey questions 13 and 15	
Disputant satisfaction with implementation	Disputant satisfaction with information and training provided to them	Disputant survey questions 10a–10c and 12a	

Table 2—continued

Research Questions and Measures	Measuring Variables	Quantitative Sources[a]	Qualitative Sources[a]
Does the ADR Program Affect Attorney Satisfaction?			
Attorney satisfaction with procedure	Attorney satisfaction with procedure measured along various dimensions including fairness, opportunity to be heard, control, and formality	Attorney survey questions 16d–16h and 17	
Attorney satisfaction with neutral	Attorney satisfaction with neutral based on competence, bias, and preparation	Attorney survey questions 18b–18g	
Attorney satisfaction with outcome	Attorney satisfaction with outcome	Attorney survey question 19	
Attorney satisfaction with implementation	Attorney satisfaction with information and training provided to them	Attorney survey questions 16a–16c and 18a	
Does the ADR Program Affect Workplace Environment?			
Relationship between disputants	Characteristics of the relationship between the disputants	Disputant survey questions 4 and 5	Interview Focus group
Number of subsequent disputes	Number of disputes	Agency records	

Table 2—continued

Research Questions and Measures	Measuring Variables	Quantitative Sources[a]	Qualitative Sources[a]
Work environment	Characteristics of the agency work environment		Interview Focus group
Management attitudes	Characteristics of agency management environment		Interview Focus group
What Are the Caseload Characteristics?			
Caseload characteristics	Number of disputes Type of disputes Type of disputants Value of disputes Complexity of disputes Background of disputants	Disputant survey questions 1–8 Attorney survey questions 1–7 Case abstraction form Sections A and B (aggregate statistics)	
Was the Program Effectively Implemented?			
Design	Consistent with applicable laws Case selection criteria Neutral selection criteria Procedural rules	Disputant survey questions 10–17 and 22–27 Attorney survey questions 16–19 Mediator survey questions 1–9 Evaluator survey questions 1–16	Review of program rules and other documentation Interview Focus Group
Education/training of agency staff	Amount of education Amount of training	Evaluator survey questions 6 and 7	Review of program rules and other documentation Interview Focus Group

Table 2—continued

Research Questions and Measures	Measuring Variables	Quantitative Sources[a]	Qualitative Sources[a]
Education/training of disputants	Amount of education Form of education Amount of training Form of training	Disputant survey questions 10a and 10b Attorney survey questions 16a and 16b Mediator survey questions 3–6	Review of program rules and other documentation Interview Focus Group
Resources	Size and education of staff Budget	Evaluator survey questions 1–3	Review of program rules and other documentation Interview Focus Group
Coordination	Coordination of office dispute resolution programs		Interview Focus group

[a]We have identified appropriate sources of data discussed in this manual and left cells blank where the source was not discussed. These are suggestions based on our experience; however, a user may identify other appropriate sources of information.

Data-Collection Instruments

This guide contains five prototype survey instruments that we have developed for evaluating an ADR program (see appendices):

- **Record Abstraction Form**
- **Evaluator Survey**
- **Disputant Survey Instrument**
- **Attorney Survey Instrument**
- **Mediator/Hearing Officer Survey Instrument.**

To develop these prototypes, we have assumed that the ADR programs being evaluated have certain common features. For example, we assume that mediation is the dispute resolution procedure and use settlement rate as an outcome measure. To adapt the prototypes for an arbitration program, simply remove mediation-specific questions and substitute relevant arbitration questions. Evaluators should adapt these instruments to their particular programs and develop supplemental materials, but as they do so, they should be sure they are linking their new information requirements back through the chain of measures to program goals.

We do not provide examples of participant interview or focus group guides. Prototypes are difficult to develop, because questions must be closely tailored to the interviewer and to the specifics of individual programs.[3]

The prototype instruments are intended to be used after cases have been resolved, since many of the data they are designed to collect will not be known until then.

Record Abstraction Form

A relatively inexpensive data-collection instrument is a record abstraction form or "face sheet" that can be attached to each case file. Important information can be entered by clerical staff as cases progress and can be collected at the time of case disposition. These data can also be abstracted from existing records at the time of the evaluation, provided that the agency's records include the needed

---

[3]Several sources may be helpful when developing qualitative data-collection instruments. They include Fowler (1984), Krueger (1988), Patton (1988), and Rossi (1979).

information. Appendix A contains a prototype Record Abstraction Form for gathering information regarding the dispute, disputants, and the procedural steps completed. Other instruments may ask some similar questions, because we have built some redundancy into the information-gathering tools to enable analysts to check the consistency and probable accuracy of some data elements before analysis.

Evaluator Survey

This form is designed to be completed by agency employees who are responsible for the ADR program evaluation and asks for information on the implementation of the ADR program. It includes objective questions on staff size, staff training, dispute selection, neutral qualification, neutral selection, and disputant education and training. Although objective questions produce responses that are easy to analyze, the responses are also less detailed and may therefore miss something of the texture that is unique to the program under evaluation. Thus, implementation may be an appropriate area for either focus groups or interviews.

Disputant Survey

The disputant survey solicits information on disputant identity, disputant satisfaction, and disputant costs. It may be difficult to identify the appropriate agency respondent. The respondent should be an agency staff member who represents the agency's interests in the case and is knowledgeable about its details. This should be less of a difficulty with private disputants.

Section A of this survey instrument asks for information regarding case type and disputant characteristics. Evaluators should expect to modify the categories in the prototype to conform to the characteristics of their caseloads. For example, if the program only handles contract disputes, it is inappropriate to include personal injury as a dispute type.

Questions 3 through 7 ask for the disputant's previous experience with ADR, the agency, and the other disputant. Previous experience may affect satisfaction with the process and therefore the success or failure of the ADR program. These questions attempt to obtain information regarding repeat disputes between the parties and therefore the effect of mediation on disputant compliance with administrative rulings.

Section B asks disputants about their satisfaction with the mediation program. In this survey, we use objective questions to quantify inherently qualitative measures. This is possible because existing research has already identified the measures that underlie disputant satisfaction. However, disputant satisfaction is also a subject where focus groups and personal interviews may help flesh out underlying nuances, interactions, and complexities.

Section C seeks information regarding the resolution of the dispute and the disputants' opinion of mediation's role in that resolution.

Section D asks disputants for information regarding their costs. We understand that costs can be a difficult variable to measure, especially for the government. However, we have designed the data-collection instruments to do the best possible job of obtaining this information. We are assuming three sources of costs for the disputants: disputant time, disputant resources, and attorneys' fees and costs. We are also assuming that the best way to compare costs is to convert all time estimates into a monetary equivalent. However, time estimates may be sufficient for comparison.

Attorney Survey

The attorney survey seeks information regarding characteristics of the dispute, information regarding the course of proceedings, attorneys' satisfaction with and perceptions of the use of mediation, and costs.

Section A asks for additional information regarding the identity of the dispute and disputants. Section B asks the attorneys to describe what actions have taken place in the dispute, and the timing of those actions.

Section C asks attorneys about their satisfaction with the mediation process. We assume that they play an important gatekeeper role with regard to ADR and mediation. Therefore, their perceptions of the process may be very important in determining the success or failure of the program.

Section D contains questions about attorneys' fees. This information duplicates information sought in the Disputant Survey. However, given the sensitivity of questions relating to fee and the problems inherent in collecting cost information generally, redundancy is appropriate.

Mediator/Hearing Officer Survey

This survey is designed for both the mediator and the hearing officer, with each filling out separate but overlapping portions. However, in many cases, no hearing officer will have been assigned. In these cases, delete those questions intended for a hearing officer.

In Sections A and B, we ask for additional information regarding the appropriateness of the dispute for mediation and the timing of the mediation. These questions repeat those contained in the disputant and attorney surveys, but they solicit a different and independent perspective on these questions.

In Section C, we ask that the respondents estimate the amount of time and the resources that they, or those in their office, spent on the dispute. These time estimates serve as surrogates for cost. The time to be reported includes time spent on preparation, research, hearings, and deliberations.[4] The survey also asks what office and administrative resources were spent on the dispute.

There is some concern that the mediators and hearing officers will be overwhelmed with forms. If hearing officers or mediators hear large numbers of suits, they will have to estimate the amount of time spent on quite a few matters over a long period of time. Unfortunately, there is very little that can be done to lighten the load.

Data Collection

The last step in the data-collection process is distributing the data-collection instruments to the designated respondents. Disputes that will be part of the study sample should be identified; then data on those cases can be collected and questionnaires can be distributed to the disputants, attorneys, and neutrals. The agency employee responsible for the ADR program evaluation should establish a collection schedule appropriate to the sampling plan and data-collection instruments. As the forms are returned, the evaluator *must* keep them well organized and ensure that all requirements to preserve their confidentiality are met.[5] To prepare for analysis, all the information that relates to each individual dispute needs to be entered and linked in an electronic database. Thus, information from a given case abstraction survey, that case's claimant, the

---

[4]To be sure we are capturing all costs, we assume here that the hearing officer and mediators are members of the agency staff. If they are not, these questions should be deleted.

[5]For a full discussion of human-subject protection requirements and ethical issues that arise in social research, see Kimmel (1989).

claimant's attorney, the respondent, the respondent's attorney, the mediator, and/or the hearing officer should all be linked.

This linked information then becomes the database for all future analysis.

4. Sample Data-Analysis Plans

The analysis plan must be developed hand-in-hand with the evaluation study design and the data-collection instruments. To help you with the development of your own plan, which will be tailored to your particular evaluation needs, we provide here three *sample* analysis plans, each addressing different policy questions. These sample analysis plans each link policy questions to outcomes and the appropriate survey items. They then suggest possible analyses.

Policy Question 1:

Does the introduction of an agency ADR program reduce the monetary costs of disputing for the agency and/or the private disputants?

Research Questions

a. What are the transaction costs for disputes in each comparison group?

b. Do the disputant and dispute characteristics differ by comparison group?

c. How is the ADR program implemented?

Analysis

The answer to the first question requires calculating and comparing the total costs borne by the parties with and without the ADR program. These costs include agency administrative costs, agency disputing costs, and private disputant costs.

All agency cost information should be compiled. Answers to Disputant Survey questions 28 through 38, Attorney Survey questions 20 through 31, Mediator/Hearing Officer Survey questions 16 through 20, and Evaluator Survey question 3 yield an estimate of total costs for the agency for each dispute. With this information, mean and median transaction costs per dispute can be calculated. Comparisons of the agency costs for disputes assigned to ADR and for those not assigned can then be made. The population not assigned might be a control group or might consist of disputes handled before the ADR program was introduced.

A similar analysis of private disputant costs can also be undertaken. Private disputant costs do not include the costs of administering the mediation program or compensating the mediator or hearing officer. Otherwise, the analysis is quite similar. The evaluator should add the costs reported in Disputant Survey questions 28 through 38 and Attorney Survey questions 20 through 31. As above, the mean and median total costs per dispute can be calculated and compared for the ADR and the non-ADR groups.

If the comparison groups differ in the kinds of disputes and/or kinds of disputants, differences in costs between the groups cannot necessarily be attributed to ADR. Thus, we need additional information on the disputant and dispute characteristics. This information can be found in Disputant Survey questions 1 through 9, Attorney Survey questions 1 through 7, and Evaluator Survey questions 1 through 16.

If dispute and disputant characteristics are similar across comparison groups, we can conclude that cost differences are related to the ADR programs. If not, we need more sophisticated analysis to identify relationships between costs and disputant and dispute characteristics. Multiple regression is one method for assessing how these various factors might relate to costs. However, application of such statistical tools will require trained technical support.

The above analysis compares the costs of the two groups. If you want to go further and explain your findings, you should incorporate implementation and case-level information into your analysis. For example, if disputes handled in the ADR program do not settle in early bilateral negotiation as frequently as those outside the program, but rather go on to mediation or some other procedure, average costs may be greater in the ADR group. Thus, this more elaborate analysis can suggest reasons for the results that are observed. The steps required for this more extensive analysis are beyond the scope of this guide.[1]

---

[1]In addition, one might speculate that disputant satisfaction also affects the costs of disputing, both for the agency and for private disputants. If disputants are satisfied with the process, they may be more likely to negotiate and mediate in good faith. If the parties pursue the settlement in good faith, time to disposition is likely to be shorter and cost less for all disputants. However, no evidence confirms or disproves such a relationship.

If evaluators want to test for a relationship, disputant satisfaction information is available through a number of sources. Disputant Survey questions 10 through 12 and Attorney Survey questions 16 through 18 provide information regarding satisfaction with the process and the mediator. In addition, Disputant Survey question 13 and Attorney Survey question 19 ask the respondents if they would use mediation again, another indication of satisfaction. Last, Disputant Survey questions 15 and 16 ask the respondents if they are satisfied with the outcome of the dispute.

Policy Question 2:

Does the introduction of an ADR program result in the more timely resolution of administrative disputes?

Research Questions

a. What is the time to disposition of disputes in the comparison groups?

b. Do the disputant and dispute characteristics differ by comparison groups?

c. How is the ADR program implemented?

Analysis

Time to disposition is the difference between the filing date and the final disposition date within the administrative proceeding. Attorney Survey questions 8 through 14 and Record Abstraction Form Section C, questions 1 through 9, and Section D, question 13 provide the needed information to calculate this period. The mean and median times to disposition for each group (those assigned and those not assigned to ADR or the "before and after" groups) can be calculated and compared.

For the reasons described in sample Policy Question 1, we also need information on disputant and dispute characteristics to determine whether or not they are similar between groups. This information can be found in Attorney Survey questions 1 through 9, Disputant Survey questions 1 through 7, and Evaluator Survey questions 1 through 16. If dispute and disputant characteristics are not the same across groups, more sophisticated analytical tools will be needed to show how these factors relate to time to disposition.

To explain your findings, you should incorporate implementation and case-level information into your analysis. For example, certain types of cases may be responsible for increasing average and median times to disposition, and identifying those types may instead suggest specific program improvements. Program implementation may be resulting in bottlenecks that are adversely affecting time to disposition.

Policy Question 3:

Does the introduction of an ADR program result in less contentious resolution of administrative disputes?

28

Research Question

Addressing this policy question is considerably more complex than addressing the last two, since the outcome of interest is *contentiousness*. An anticipated benefit of the introduction of ADR is that the disputing environment will become less contentious, and the further hope is that a less contentious disputing environment will lead to a less adversarial and contentious work environment. Measuring reductions, however, can be extremely problematic, since there is no obvious measure for "contentiousness" as there is for cost and for time to disposition. In this sample analysis plan, we propose two types of approaches: a quantitative approach and a qualitative approach.

Quantitative Approach. A quantitative approach rests on a number of questions, each probing a possible component of "contentiousness." Assuming a Before and After design, they are as follows:

a. Are there fewer disputes in the ADR group than the comparison group?

b. Are there fewer recurring disputes in the ADR group than in the comparison group?

c. Are there fewer new disputes between the same parties in the ADR group than in the comparison group?

d. Are there more settlements in the ADR group than in the comparison group?

e. Is the time to disposition shorter in the ADR group than in the comparison group?

f. Are disputants in the ADR group more satisfied with the process and outcomes than those in the comparison group?

Each of these questions has an underlying logic that relates to the contentiousness of the environment.

New and recurring disputes. In a less contentious disputing environment, we might expect that aggrieved parties will settle more of their disputes outside of any formal complaint arena and that there will be fewer recurring disputes. Thus, if this is true, fewer disputes should be recorded subsequent to the implementation of the ADR program.

Compliance with awards and agreements. In a less contentious disputing environment, disputants should be more likely to comply with the awards or agreements that result from the process; hence, we will observe fewer recurring disputes.

Disputes between the same parties. Similarly, settlements or other forms of dispute resolution will more permanently heal the breach between disputants, and there should be fewer new disputes between the same parties.

Time to disposition and costs. In less contentious environments, it is likely that time to disposition and costs will be less, since disputants will be less adversarial.

Satisfaction with the process. Disputants who are satisfied with the process they have experienced can be expected to be less contentious and adversarial in the future.

Qualitative Approach. Qualitative methods may also contribute substantially to an understanding of the effects of ADR on "contentiousness," both because perceptions may be a significant factor in determining contentiousness and because qualitative methods are useful in exploring complex causal links.[2] A qualitative approach might rest on a two-step process: (1) exploratory interviewing to identify the factors that participants in the process think contribute to and/or reflect contentiousness and (2) focus groups and open-ended interviewing based on information gained in the exploratory phase to determine how the introduction of ADR affects contentiousness.

Analysis

Since this guide only provides prototype instruments that support a quantitative approach, our sample analysis also limits itself to that approach.

Answering each of the research questions separately is straightforward and follows the same model set forth in Policy Questions 1 and 2. The numbers of disputes in the comparison groups can be calculated from the administrative record data. The numbers of recurring disputes and disputes between the same parties can be calculated from the names listed in the record abstraction data file. In addition, Disputant Survey questions 3 through 7 ask disputants for information regarding previous disputes. The number of disputes that settle is available from question 10 of the Record Abstraction Form, Section A. As indicated above, time to disposition can be calculated from the filing date and the final disposition date available from both the Record Abstraction Form and the Attorney Survey. Finally, information characterizing disputant satisfaction is available from a number of sources. Disputant Survey questions 10 through 12 and Attorney Survey questions 16 through 19 provide information regarding satisfaction with the process and the mediator. In addition, Disputant Survey

---

[2]See Section 2.

question 13 and Attorney Survey question 19 ask respondents if they would use mediation again, and Disputant Survey questions 15 and 16 ask if they are satisfied with the outcome of the dispute.

Unfortunately, answers to each of the individual research questions cannot be readily aggregated into an overall measure of contentiousness. This step is difficult and requires a more comprehensive analysis than can be set forth here.

5. Presenting the Results

The results of the evaluation data collection and analysis will ultimately have to be crystallized and presented, usually in an evaluation report or briefing. How the results are presented may be as important to the acceptance and use of the evaluation as the study itself. Evaluators should pay particular attention to

- **Accurately reporting the findings of their analyses**
- **Noting the limitations of methods they may use**
- **Presenting data in a clear, preferably graphic, form**
- **Developing their presentation to conform to the broad policy dimensions along which the program is being evaluated.**

And finally, results should be presented in a timely fashion, so they are not outdated.

Appendix

A. Record Abstraction Form

Introduction

This survey is designed to gather data regarding disputant identification, disputant characteristics, and the timing of dispute proceedings. It, and the following survey, should be completed by the agency employee(s) responsible for the evaluation of the ADR program.

This survey will need to be adapted to reflect the particular types of disputants and proceedings in the program being evaluated. For example, if insurance companies play a prominent role in the program being evaluated, a disputant type "insurance company" may be added. Further, if the program being evaluated is, for example, a neutral-evaluation program, the questions regarding the dispute proceedings should reflect that fact.

RECORD ABSTRACTION FORM

A. Disputant Identification

1. Dispute Name: _____ v. _____

   _____   _____

2. Complaint Date:

  MO | DAY | YR

Code up to 3 claimants in this dispute. If there are more than 3 claimants, list name, counsel, and type, on the last page of this section.

I. CLAIMANTS OR COMPLAINANTS

	Claimant #1
3. Claimant Name	First Name MI Last Name **OR** _____ Corporate/Institution Name
4. Claimant Counsel	☐ Pro Se (Provide Claimant name and address below.) ☐ Not Reported Counsel Name _____ Firm Name Street/PO Box City State Zip ( ) Area Code Phone Number

Claimant #2	Claimant #3
First Name MI Last Name	First Name MI Last Name
O R	**O R**
Corporate/Institution Name	Corporate/Institution Name

Claimant #2:

☐ Pro Se (Provide Claimant name and address below.)

☐ Not Reported

Same as Claimant # ☐

Counsel Name

Firm Name

Street/PO Box

City   State Zip

(   )
Area Code   Phone Number

Claimant #3:

☐ Pro Se (Provide Claimant name and address below.)

☐ Not Reported

Same as Claimant # ☐

Counsel Name

Firm Name

Street/PO Box

City   State Zip

(   )
Area Code   Phone Number

36

II. RESPONDENTS

Code up to 3 respondents in this dispute. If there are more than 3 respondents, list name, counsel, type and insurance information on the last page of this section.

Respondent   #1

5. Respondent Name	First Name MI Last Name
	OR
	Corporate/Institution Name

	☐ Pro Se (Provide Respondent name and address below.)
	☐ Not Reported
	Counsel Name
6. Respondent Counsel	Firm Name
	Street/PO Box
	City State Zip
	( )
	Area Code Phone Number

Respondent #2	Respondent #3
First Name MI Last Name	First Name MI Last Name
OR	OR
Corporate/Institution Name	Corporate/Institution Name

Respondent #2	Respondent #3
☐ Pro Se (Provide Respondent name and address below.)	☐ Pro Se (Provide Respondent name and address below.)
☐ Not Reported	☐ Not Reported
Same as Respondent # ☐	Same as Respondent # ☐
Counsel Name	Counsel Name
Firm Name	Firm Name
Street/PO Box	Street/PO Box
City State Zip	City State Zip
( )	( )
Area Code Phone Number	Area Code Phone Number

38

B. Disputant Types

COMPLETE FOR EACH DISPUTANT LISTED IN SECTION A.

I. CLAIMANT TYPE	II. RESPONDENT TYPE

1. Claimant #1

(CHECK ONE)

- ☐ 1 Private individual
- ☐ 2 Small business owner (less than 10 employees)
- ☐ 3 Larger business owner (10 employees or more)
- ☐ 4 Professional individual
- ☐ 5 Business employee or officer
- ☐ 6 Public agency employee
- ☐ 7 NOT REPORTED

1. Respondent #1

(CHECK ONE)

- ☐ 1 Private individual
- ☐ 2 Small business owner (less than 10 employees)
- ☐ 3 Larger business owner (10 employees or more)
- ☐ 4 Professional individual
- ☐ 5 Business employee or officer
- ☐ 6 Public agency employee
- ☐ 7 NOT REPORTED

2. Claimant #2

(CHECK ONE)

- ☐ 1 Private individual
- ☐ 2 Small business owner (less than 10 employees)
- ☐ 3 Larger business owner (10 employees or more)
- ☐ 4 Professional individual
- ☐ 5 Business employee or officer
- ☐ 6 Public agency employee
- ☐ 7 NOT REPORTED

2. Respondent #2

(CHECK ONE)

- ☐ 1 Private individual
- ☐ 2 Small business owner (less than 10 employees)
- ☐ 3 Larger business owner (10 employees or more)
- ☐ 4 Professional individual
- ☐ 5 Business employee or officer
- ☐ 6 Public agency employee
- ☐ 7 NOT REPORTED

3. Claimant #3

(CHECK ONE)

- ☐ 1 Private individual
- ☐ 2 Small business owner (less than 10 employees)
- ☐ 3 Larger business owner (10 employees or more)
- ☐ 4 Professional individual
- ☐ 5 Business employee or officer
- ☐ 6 Public agency employee
- ☐ 7 NOT REPORTED

3. Respondent #3

(CHECK ONE)

- ☐ 1 Private individual
- ☐ 2 Small business owner (less than 10 employees)
- ☐ 3 Larger business owner (10 employees or more)
- ☐ 4 Professional individual
- ☐ 5 Business employee or officer
- ☐ 6 Public agency employee
- ☐ 7 NOT REPORTED

C. Dispute Proceedings

1. When was the administrative complaint filed?

_____ / _____   **OR**   ☐ 9 NOT REPORTED
   MONTH   YEAR

2. When was an answer filed?

_____ / _____   **OR**   ☐ 8 NOT ANSWERED
   MONTH   YEAR   ☐ 9 NOT REPORTED

3 When did discovery begin?

_____ / _____   **OR**   ☐ 8 NO DISCOVERY
   MONTH   YEAR   ☐ 9 NOT REPORTED

4. When were prehearing motions filed?

_____ / _____   **OR**   ☐ 8 NO MOTIONS
   MONTH   YEAR   ☐ 9 NOT REPORTED

5. Was this dispute mediated through (AGENCY)'s ADR program?

   (CHECK ONE)

   ☐ 1 Yes
   ☐ 2 No ⇒ <u>Skip to Question 10. Next page</u>

6. When was the mediation session held?

_____ / _____   **OR**   ☐ 9 NOT REPORTED
   MONTH   YEAR

7. What is the name of the neutral?

_____
   First   Last

8. Was this neutral:

    (CHECK ONE)

    ☐ 1   (AGENCY) personnel
    ☐ 2   Another agency personnel
    ☐ 3   Non-government personnel

___

9. What was the outcome of mediation?

    (CHECK ONE)

    ☐ 1   Case settled
    ☐ 2   Case was NOT settled
    ☐ 9   NOT REPORTED

___

10. Was an administrative hearing held in this dispute?

    (CHECK ONE)

    ☐ 1   Yes
    ☐ 2   No ⇒ <u>Skip to Section D</u>

11. When was the administrative hearing held?

    _____/_____   **OR**   ☐ 9   NOT REPORTED
    MONTH   YEAR

___

D. Final Outcome of Dispute

12. What is the final outcome of this dispute?

    (CHECK ONE)

    ☐ 1   No final outcome, dispute still active ⇒ <u>Skip to END, Next page</u>
    ☐ 2   Dispute settled BEFORE hearing or mediation ⇒ <u>Skip to Question 15, Next page</u>
    ☐ 3   Administrative hearing judgment
    ☐ 4   Dispute settled AT mediation ⇒ <u>Skip to Question 15, Next page</u>
    ☐ 5   Dispute settled AFTER hearing or mediation ⇒ <u>Skip to Question 15, Next page</u>
    ☐ 6   Other outcome (specify):_____ ⇒ <u>Skip to Question 15, Next page</u>
    ☐ 9   NOT REPORTED ⇒ <u>Skip to Question 15, Next page</u>

___

13. What was the administrative hearing judgment?

(CHECK ONE)

☐ 1   No cause/respondent judgment ⇒ <u>Skip to Question 15</u>

☐ 2   Judgment for claimant or cross-claimant

☐ 3   Other (specify):_____ ⇒ <u>Skip to Question 15</u>

☐ 9   NOT REPORTED ⇒ <u>Skip to Question 15</u>

14. Please record the judgment below:

(CHECK ONE)

☐ 1   Monetary judgment ⇒ TOTAL AWARD:$_____ .00

☐ 2   Non monetary judgment

☐ 9   NOT REPORTED

_____

15. What is the date of the final outcome of this dispute?

_____ / _____   **OR**   ☐ 9   NOT REPORTED
MONTH   YEAR

```
┌─────────────────────────────────────────────────┐
│      END:  THIS COMPLETES THE CASE ABSTRACTION.   │
└─────────────────────────────────────────────────┘
```

B. Evaluator Survey

Introduction

This survey is designed to gather data regarding the ADR program, including its size, budget, case selection rules, neutral selection rules, educational programs, and training procedures. It should be completed by the agency employee(s) responsible for the evaluation of the ADR program.

This survey may need to be adapted to reflect the particular program designs, rules, or structures. In addition, the agency may wish to get additional information regarding these features through interviews or focus groups to further develop this particular survey instrument.

Evaluator Survey

1. How many cases have been assigned to the mediation program in the past year?

    ☐☐☐☐ CASES

2. How many staff (not including mediators) are assigned to the mediation program? AGENCY DEFINITION OF STAFF MAY VARY (E.G. FTE, INDIVIDUALS, ETC.)

    ☐☐☐☐ STAFF

3. What was the total budget (NOT including mediators) for this agency's mediation program last year?

    TOTAL $:_____ .00

4. Is there a training program for agency staff (not including mediators) involved in the ADR program?

    (CHECK ONE)

    ☐₁ Yes
    ☐₂ No

5. Are all offices of this agency participating in the ADR program, or is the program limited to one agency office?

    (CHECK ONE)

    ☐₁ All offices
    ☐₂ More than one, but not all
    ☐₃ Limited to one office

44

6. What procedures exist to give the disputants information about the mediation program?

   (CHECK ALL THAT APPLY)

   ☐ 1 None at this time
   ☐ 2 Information included only in agency administrative rules
   ☐ 3 Information included in supplemental written form
   ☐ 4 Disputants orally informed of program
   ☐ 5 Disputants offered mediation seminars
   ☐ 6 Other, specify:_____

7. What procedures exist to provide the disputants with training in mediation techniques?

   (CHECK ALL THAT APPLY)

   ☐ 1 None at this time
   ☐ 2 Disputants given written materials
   ☐ 3 Disputants offered seminars
   ☐ 4 Other (specify):_____

8. Are there case selection procedures?

   (CHECK ONE)

   ☐ 1 Yes, systematic selection
   ☐ 2 Yes, staff select on a case-by-case basis
   ☐ 3 Yes, judge selects on a case-by-case basis
   ☐ 4 Yes, some other procedure (specify):_____
   ☐ 5 No

9. After being selected for the mediation program, do the disputants have the option of refusing mediation?

   (CHECK ONE)

   ☐ 1 Yes
   ☐ 2 No

10. Does the program maintain a list of neutrals to act as mediators?

   (CHECK ONE)

   ☐ 1   Yes
   ☐ 2   No ⟹ <u>Skip to Question 11</u>

   10A.   Do neutrals have to meet certain qualifications to be on this list?

   (CHECK ONE)

   ☐ 1   Yes
   ☐ 2   No

11. Do agency personnel serve as neutrals?

   (CHECK ONE)

   ☐ 1   Yes
   ☐ 2   No

12. Do outside personnel serve as neutrals?

   (CHECK ONE)

   ☐ 1   Yes
   ☐ 2   No

13. Do neutrals receive training?

   (CHECK ONE)

   ☐ 1   Yes
   ☐ 2   No ⟹ <u>Skip to Question 14</u>

   13A. Are neutrals required to receive training?

   (CHECK ONE)

   ☐ 1   Yes
   ☐ 2   No

14. Is the neutral chosen by the disputants?

    (CHECK ONE)

    ☐ 1 Yes ⟹ <u>Skip to END</u>
    ☐ 2 No

15. Is the neutral chosen by the program staff (including the administrative judge)?

    (CHECK ONE)

    ☐ 1 Yes
    ☐ 2 No ⟹ <u>Skip to END</u>

16. Do the disputants have the opportunity to accept or reject the chosen neutral?

    (CHECK ONE)

    ☐ 1 Yes
    ☐ 2 No

END: This completes the Evaluation Officer Survey

C. Disputant Survey

Introduction

This survey is designed to gather data regarding the disputants, their past experience with administrative proceedings and ADR, their satisfaction with the ADR program under evaluation, the resolution of the dispute, and their costs. This survey should be completed by a disputant or disputant officer with sufficient knowledge to fully answer all questions.

This survey may need to be adapted to reflect the particular characteristics of the program being evaluated. For example, questions should be appropriate for the particular types of disputants using the program being evaluated. If insurance companies play a prominent role in the program being evaluated, a disputant type "insurance company" should be added. In addition, additional categories of costs in particular types of disputes may need to be incorporated into the cost calculation.

Disputant Survey

Instructions:

- Please answer each question by checking the appropriate box or filling in a number.

- Skip questions only if you are instructed to do so.

- Please be assured that the information you provide will be kept strictly confidential.

- When you have completed this questionnaire, please place it in the envelope provided and (INSERT AGENCY SPECIFIC INSTRUCTIONS).

Thank you for your assistance.

A. Background
First, a few questions about you.

1. Were you a claimant or respondent in this dispute? (The claimant is the party filing the complaint while the respondent is the party the claim is filed against.)

   (CHECK ONE)

   ☐ 1 Claimant
   ☐ 2 Respondent

2. Were you involved in this dispute as a private individual, or as an employee or officer of an organization?

   (CHECK ONE)

   ☐ 1 Private individual
   ☐ 2 Small business owner (less than 10 employees)
   ☐ 3 Larger business owner (10 employees or more)
   ☐ 4 Professional individual
   ☐ 5 Business employee or officer
   ☐ 6 Public agency employee

3. Have you ever been involved in an administrative proceeding before?

    (CHECK ONE)

    ☐ 1 Yes
    ☐ 2 No ⇒ <u>Skip to Question 7</u>

4. Did any past administrative proceeding include the <u>same</u> opposing party as this current dispute?

    (CHECK ONE)

    ☐ 1 Yes
    ☐ 2 No ⇒ <u>Skip to Question 6</u>

5. Was that past administrative proceeding related to this current dispute or was it about a <u>different</u> matter?

    (CHECK ONE)

    ☐ 1 Current dispute
    ☐ 2 Different matter

6. Have you ever been involved before as a party with <u>this agency's</u> ADR program?

    (CHECK ONE)

    ☐ 1 Yes
    ☐ 2 No

7. Have you ever been involved before as a party with <u>another</u> ADR program?

    (CHECK ONE)

    ☐ 1 Yes
    ☐ 2 No

50

8. When did this particular dispute begin?

_____/_____   **OR**   ☐ 9 Don't know
MONTH   YEAR

9. In this dispute, were you represented by:

   (CHECK ONE)

   ☐ 1 A private lawyer
   ☐ 2 Your employer's lawyer
   ☐ 3 (AGENCY) lawyer
   ☐ 4 NO LAWYER--REPRESENTED MYSELF
   ☐ 5 Other
   Please specify:_____

10. Was this dispute mediated through (AGENCY)'s ADR program?

   (CHECK ONE)

   ☐ 1 Yes
   ☐ 2 No ⇒ <u>Skip to Question 15, Page 5</u>

B. Satisfaction With Mediation

11. Please indicate how satisfied you were with each of the following features of mediation:

(CHECK ONE ON EACH LINE)

	Very Satisfied	Somewhat Satisfied	Neither	Somewhat Dissatisfied	Very Dissatisfied	Does Not Apply
a. The amount of information (AGENCY) gave you about mediation.	☐1	☐2	☐3	☐4	☐5	☐6
b. The amount of mediation training (AGENCY) gave you.	☐1	☐2	☐3	☐4	☐5	☐6
c. How your case was selected for mediation.	☐1	☐2	☐3	☐4	☐5	
d. The amount of control you had over the way the mediation was conducted.	☐1	☐2	☐3	☐4	☐5	
e. The opportunity you had to present your side of the case.	☐1	☐2	☐3	☐4	☐5	
f. The fairness of the mediation.	☐1	☐2	☐3	☐4	☐5	
g. Your level of participation in the mediation.	☐1	☐2	☐3	☐4	☐5	
h. Overall process.	☐1	☐2	☐3	☐4	☐5	

12. How much do you agree or disagree with the following statements about the mediation?

(CHECK ONE)

	Strongly Agree	Mostly Agree	Mostly Disagree	Strongly Disagree
a. The mediation session was too formal.	☐1	☐2	☐3	☐4
b. The mediation session was too informal.	☐1	☐2	☐3	☐4

13. How satisfied you were with each of the following features or qualities of the mediator?

(CHECK ONE ON EACH LINE)

	Very Satisfied	Somewhat Satisfied	Neither	Somewhat Dissatisfied	Very Dissatisfied
a. How the mediator was selected.	☐ 1	☐ 2	☐ 3	☐ 4	☐ 5
b. How prepared the mediator was to hear this dispute.........................	☐ 1	☐ 2	☐ 3	☐ 4	☐ 5
c. The amount of respect the mediator gave you...........................	☐ 1	☐ 2	☐ 3	☐ 4	☐ 5
d. How knowledgeable the mediator was about the substance and law of this dispute...........................	☐ 1	☐ 2	☐ 3	☐ 4	☐ 5
e. The fairness of the mediator.	☐ 1	☐ 2	☐ 3	☐ 4	☐ 5
f. The mediator's skill in working with all disputants to reach an agreement.	☐ 1	☐ 2	☐ 3	☐ 4	☐ 5
g. The mediator overall..............................	☐ 1	☐ 2	☐ 3	☐ 4	☐ 5

14. Assuming you had the choice, would you use mediation to solve future disputes under similar circumstances?

(CHECK ONE)

☐ 1 Yes
☐ 2 No
☐ 3 Don't Know

C. Resolution Of Dispute

15. Now we would like you to think about the resolution of this dispute. Do you think that you (or your organization) won or lost?

(CHECK ONE)

☐ 1 Won
☐ 2 Lost
☐ 3 Mixed result
☐ 4 Don't know

53

16. How satisfied were you with the resolution of this dispute?

    (CHECK ONE)

    ☐₁ Very satisfied
    ☐₂ Somewhat satisfied
    ☐₂ Neither satisfied nor dissatisfied
    ☐₄ Somewhat dissatisfied
    ☐₅ Very dissatisfied

17. How fair do you think the resolution of this dispute was for you (or your organization)?

    (CHECK ONE)

    ☐₁ Very fair
    ☐₂ Somewhat fair
    ☐₃ Somewhat unfair
    ☐₄ Very unfair

18. Was any money at stake in this dispute?

    (CHECK ONE)

    ☐₁ Yes
    ☐₂ No ⇒ <u>Skip to Question 19, Page 7</u>

19. What was the total dollar amount of the final settlement and/or award for or against you (or your organization) in this dispute?

    IF YOU (OR YOUR ORGANIZATION) RECEIVED OR WILL RECEIVE MONEY IN SETTLEMENT OR AWARD: Do not subtract your (or your organization's) legal fees and expenses from the amount reported below.

    RECEIVE $_____.00

    IF YOU (OR YOUR INSURER) PAID OR WILL PAY MONEY IN SETTLEMENT OR AWARD: Do not include your (or your organization's) legal fees and expenses in the amount reported below.

    PAY $_____.00

54

20. Were any non-monetary stakes involved in this dispute (for example you or another party being asked to do something or stop doing something that didn't involve money)?

(CHECK ONE)

☐ 1 Yes

☐ 2 No

21. Was there any non-monetary outcome that resulted from this dispute (for example, an order from the administrative judge, or a non-monetary substantive agreement between disputants)?

(CHECK ONE)

☐ 1 Yes, a non-monetary order from the administrative judge

☐ 2 Yes, a non-monetary substantive agreement between disputants

☐ 3 No

22. Please check the statement below that best matches the resolution of this dispute.

(CHECK ONE)

☐ 1 This dispute was NOT mediated, and NO settlement was reached. ⇒ <u>Skip to Question 27, Page 9</u>

☐ 2 This dispute was NOT mediated, AND a settlement was reached. ⇒ <u>Skip to Question 27, Page 9</u>

☐ 3 This dispute was mediated, but NO settlement was reached. ⇒ <u>Skip to Question 25, next page</u>

☐ 4 This dispute was mediated, AND a settlement was reached.

23. Did mediation help reach a settlement in less time than an administrative hearing would have taken?

(CHECK ONE)

☐ 1 Yes

☐ 2 No

☐ 3 Don't Know

24. Did you (or your organization) save resources such as staff time or other costs by using mediation?

(CHECK ONE)

☐₁ Yes
☐₂ No
☐₃ Don't Know

PLEASE SKIP TO QUESTION 26.
---

25. Even though mediation failed to result in settlement, were there other positive outcomes (such as a better understanding of the issue or better communications between the disputants)?

(CHECK ONE)

☐₁ Yes
☐₂ No ⇒ Skip to Question 26

25A. What were the positive outcomes?

(CHECK ALL THAT APPLY)

☐₁ Partial settlement
☐₂ Other
Please specify:_____

26. Was the timing of the mediation appropriate for it to contribute positively to the resolution of this dispute, or would the mediation have been more productive if it were held earlier or later in the process?

(CHECK ONE)

☐₁ Should have mediated earlier
☐₂ Right time
☐₃ Should have mediated later

PLEASE SKIP TO SECTION D, PAGE 9

56

27. Although mediation was not used in this dispute, do you think mediation would have helped reach a settlement in less time than an administrative hearing?

(CHECK ONE)

☐₁ Yes
☐₂ No
☐₃ Don't Know

28. Do you think mediation would have saved you (or your organization) resources such as staff time or other costs compared to an administrative hearing?

(CHECK ONE)

☐₁ Yes
☐₂ No
☐₃ Don't Know

D. Costs
In order to understand the economic costs of disputes, we need as much information as possible about costs to you (or your organization) associated with this dispute. We realize records and other information related to costs may not be available. In answering the questions in this section, please give us your best estimate of the actual amounts.

29. Please check the statement below that best describes you.

(CHECK ONE)

☐₁ I am answering this questionnaire as an individual.
☐₂ I am answering this questionnaire for my organization ⇒ Skip to Question 33, Page 11

30. Altogether, how many hours did you spend on the legal aspects of this dispute? Include time spent talking with lawyers or experts, appearing at mediation or administrative hearings, being deposed, collecting information, and filling out forms, but do not include time discussing the case with family and friends.

TOTAL HOURS _____

31. Which category below, best matches your salary or business income for last year?

(CHECK ONE)

☐ 1   Less than $20,000
☐ 2 $20,000 - $35,000
☐ 3 $36,000 - $40,000
☐ 4 $41,000 - $55,000
☐ 5 $56,000 - $70,000
☐ 6   More than $70,000

32. What were the TOTAL legal fees and expenses you paid (or will pay) in this case, including lawyers' fees, expert witness fees, transcript fees, and fees for legal assistants, paralegals, or investigators? Do not include the costs of medical treatment or lost earnings while injured, or the premiums paid for prepaid legal insurance (if any). Remember, your best estimate is fine.

TOTAL FEES AND EXPENSES $_____.00

THANK YOU FOR YOUR ASSISTANCE. PLEASE PLACE THIS FORM IN THE ENVELOPE PROVIDED AND (INSERT AGENCY SPECIFIC INSTRUCTIONS HERE).

58

33. Excluding time spent by lawyers, think how many hours IN TOTAL were spent by all individuals in your organization on the legal aspects of this dispute. Please record below the time spent by in-house experts, clerical staff, administrative staff and all other personnel in your organization on this dispute. Include time spent talking with lawyers or experts, appearing at mediation or administrative hearings, being deposed, collecting information, and filling out paper work. Your best estimate of the total is fine.

GOVERNMENT AGENCIES:

(INSERT HOURS BY PAY GRADE LIST HERE)

ALL OTHER ORGANIZATIONS:

WAGE OF STAFF	TOTAL HOURS ALL STAFF AT THIS WAGE
Less than $10 an hour	_____
$10 - $20 an hour	_____
$20 - $40 an hour	_____
$40- $60 an hour	_____
$60 - $80 an hour	_____
$80 - $100 an hour	_____
More than $100 an hour	_____

34. If applicable, what was the highest level of officer in your organization involved in the resolution of this dispute?

TITLE: _____

35. Did any salaried or pre-paid lawyers such as government lawyers, private lawyers who were salaried employees of your organization, or prepaid legal plan lawyers work for your organization on this dispute?

(CHECK ONE)

☐ 1 Yes
☐ 2 No ⇒ Skip to Question 39, Page 12

36. What was the approximate TOTAL number of hours that all government lawyers, private lawyers who were salaried employees of the organization, or prepaid legal plan lawyers worked on this case?

TOTAL SALARIED OR
PRE-PAID LAWYER HOURS _____

37. Please break down the total number of hours worked by pre-paid or salaried lawyers into each of the salary categories listed below. Again, your best estimate will do.

YEARLY SALARY	NUMBER OF HOURS
Less than $50,000	_____
$50,000 - $75,000	_____
$76,000 - $100,000	_____
$101,000 - $125,000	_____
More than $125,000	_____

38. For these government, other salaried, or prepaid legal plan lawyers, please estimate all NON-SALARY expenses such as any non-salary staff or experts, investigations, filing fees, transcript fees, copying expenses, and exhibit costs that were paid (or will be paid) by your organization.

TOTAL EXPENSES FOR
SALARIED/PRE-PAID LAWYERS $_____.00

39. Not including the costs and expenses you may have reported in Q.37 and 38, please estimate the legal fees and expenses your organization paid (or will pay). Remember, your best estimate will do.

TOTAL LEGAL
FEES AND EXPENSES $_____.00

THANK YOU FOR YOUR ASSISTANCE. PLEASE PLACE THIS FORM IN THE ENVELOPE PROVIDED AND (INSERT AGENCY SPECIFIC INSTRUCTIONS HERE).

D. Attorney Survey

Introduction

This survey is designed to gather data regarding the types of disputants, types of disputes, the complexity of the disputes, the attorney's past experience with administrative proceedings and ADR, the attorney's satisfaction with the ADR program under evaluation, the timing of dispute proceedings, and the attorney's fees. This survey should be completed by an attorney with sufficient knowledge of the dispute to fully answer all questions.

This survey may need to be adapted to reflect the particular characteristics of the program being evaluated, including the particular types of disputants, types of disputes, and dispute proceedings in the program being evaluated. For example, if insurance companies play a prominent role in the program being evaluated, a disputant type "insurance company" may be added. In addition, other categories of attorneys' fees that are involved in particular types of disputes may need to be incorporated into the cost calculation.

Attorney Survey

> **Instructions:**
>
> - Please answer each question by checking the appropriate box or filling in a number.
>
> - Skip questions only if you are instructed to do so.
>
> - Please be assured that the information you provide will be kept strictly confidential.
>
> - When you have completed this questionnaire, please place it in the envelope provided and (INSERT AGENCY SPECIFIC INSTRUCTIONS).
>
> Thank you for your assistance.

A. Background

1. Did you represent the claimant or respondent in this dispute?

    (CHECK ONE)

    ☐₁ Claimant
    ☐₂ Respondent

2. Is your client a private individual, or an employee or officer of an organization?

    (CHECK ONE)

    ☐₁ Private individual
    ☐₂ Small business owner (less than 10 employees)
    ☐₃ Larger business owner (10 employees or more)
    ☐₄ Professional individual
    ☐₅ Business employee or officer
    ☐₆ Public agency employee

3. Have you ever represented a disputant involved in an administrative proceeding before?

    (CHECK ONE)

    ☐₁ Yes
    ☐₂ No ⇒ <u>Skip to Question 5</u>

62

4. Have you ever represented a disputant in <u>this</u> <u>agency's</u> ADR program?

    (CHECK ONE)

    ☐₁ Yes
    ☐₂ No

5. Have you ever represented a disputant in <u>any other agency's</u> ADR program?

    (CHECK ONE)

    ☐₁ Yes
    ☐₂ No

6. Which category below best describes this dispute?

    (CHECK ONE)

    ☐₁ Breach of contract
    ☐₂ Personal injury
    ☐₃ Employment
    ☐₄ Environmental
    ☐₅ Other
        Please specify:_____

7. When your involvement in this dispute began, how would you have rated each of the factors below?

(CHECK ONE ON EACH LINE)

	More than Average	Average	Less than Average
a. Overall complexity of the dispute.	☐1	☐2	☐3
b. The difficulty of discovery in this dispute.	☐1	☐2	☐3
c. The complexity of the legal issues involved in this dispute.	☐1	☐2	☐3
d. The difficulty in relations between the disputants.	☐1	☐2	☐3
e. The disparity in position between the disputants.	☐1	☐2	☐3

B. Procedures Employed

8. When did this dispute begin?

_____ / _____
  MONTH   YEAR

9. Was this dispute mediated?

(CHECK ONE)

☐1 Yes ⇒ When was the (first) mediation session held? _____ / _____
☐2 No   MONTH   YEAR

10. When was the administrative complaint filed?

_____ / _____
  MONTH   YEAR

- 3 -

64

11. Was an answer filed?

   (CHECK ONE)

   ☐₁ Yes ⇒ When was it filed? _____ /_____
   ☐₂ No   MONTH   YEAR

12 Did discovery begin?

   (CHECK ONE)

   ☐₁ Yes ⇒ When did it begin? _____ /_____
   ☐₂ No   MONTH   YEAR

13. Were prehearing motions filed?

   (CHECK ONE)

   ☐₁ Yes ⇒ When (first) filed? _____ /_____
   ☐₂ No   MONTH   YEAR

14. Was an administrative hearing held in this dispute?

   (CHECK ONE)

   ☐₁ Yes ⇒ When was it held? _____ /_____
   ☐₂ No   MONTH   YEAR

15. Was this dispute mediated through (AGENCY)'s ADR program?

 (CHECK ONE)

 ☐ ₁ Yes
 ☐ ₂ No ⇒ <u>Skip to Section D, Page 7</u>

C. Satisfaction With Mediation

16. Please indicate how satisfied you were with each of the following features of mediation:

(CHECK ONE ON EACH LINE)

	Very Satisfied	Somewhat Satisfied	Neither	Somewhat Dissatisfied	Very Dissatisfied	Does Not Apply
a. The amount of information (AGENCY) gave you about mediation.	☐ 1	☐ 2	☐ 3	☐ 4	☐ 5	☐ 6
b. The amount of mediation training (AGENCY) gave you.	☐ 1	☐ 2	☐ 3	☐ 4	☐ 5	☐ 6
c. How your case was selected for mediation.	☐ 1	☐ 2	☐ 3	☐ 4	☐ 5	
d. The amount of control you had over the way the mediation was conducted.	☐ 1	☐ 2	☐ 3	☐ 4	☐ 5	
e. The opportunity you had to present your side of the case.	☐ 1	☐ 2	☐ 3	☐ 4	☐ 5	
f The fairness of the mediation.	☐ 1	☐ 2	☐ 3	☐ 4	☐ 5	
g. Your level of participation in the mediation.	☐ 1	☐ 2	☐ 3	☐ 4	☐ 5	
h. Overall process.	☐ 1	☐ 2	☐ 3	☐ 4	☐ 5	

66

17. How much do you agree or disagree with the following statements about the mediation?

(CHECK ONE)

	Strongly Agree	Mostly Agree	Mostly Disagree	Strongly Disagree
a. The mediation session was too <u>formal</u>.	☐ 1	☐ 2	☐ 3	☐ 4
b. The mediation session was too <u>informal</u>.	☐ 1	☐ 2	☐ 3	☐ 4

18. Please indicate how satisfied you were with each of the following features or qualities of the mediator?

(CHECK ONE ON EACH LINE)

	Very Satisfied	Somewhat Satisfied	<u>Neither</u>	Somewhat Dissatisfied	Very Dissatisfied
a. How the mediator was selected.	☐ 1	☐ 2	☐ 3	☐ 4	☐ 5
b. How prepared the mediator was to hear this dispute	☐ 1	☐ 2	☐ 3	☐ 4	☐ 5
c. The amount of respect the mediator gave you	☐ 1	☐ 2	☐ 3	☐ 4	☐ 5
d. How knowledgeable the mediator was about the substance and law of this dispute	☐ 1	☐ 2	☐ 3	☐ 4	☐ 5
e. The fairness of the mediator.	☐ 1	☐ 2	☐ 3	☐ 4	☐ 5
f. The mediator's skill in working with all disputants to reach an agreement.	☐ 1	☐ 2	☐ 3	☐ 4	☐ 5
g. The mediator overall	☐ 1	☐ 2	☐ 3	☐ 4	☐ 5

19. Assuming you had the choice, would you use mediation to solve future disputes under similar circumstances?

(CHECK ONE)

☐ 1 Yes
☐ 2 No
☐ 3 Don't Know

D. Costs

In order to understand the economic costs of disputes, we need as much information as possible about costs associated with <u>this</u> dispute. We realize records and other information related to costs may not be available. In answering the questions in this section, please give us your best estimate of the actual amounts.

20. Please check the statement below that best describes you.

     (CHECK ONE)

     ☐₁ I have billed (or will bill) my client
          for all fees and costs associated with this dispute.

     ☐₂ I worked on this dispute on a salaried or pre-paid basis.⇒ <u>Skip to Question 28, Page 9</u>

21. We would like you to provide the approximate number of hours worked by ALL attorneys representing your client or your client's side of this dispute -- including government agency attorneys, in-house counsel, salaried attorneys employed insurers, and all other attorneys associated with your client's side of this dispute. Can you provide an estimate of this total?

     (CHECK ONE)

     ☐₁ Yes, I can provide an estimate for all attorneys combined ⇒ <u>Skip to Question 23 Next page</u>

     ☐₂ No, I can only estimate my time and can NOT provide
          an estimate of the time spent by other attorneys on my client's side of the dispute.

22. Please print the names and addresses of attorneys you can NOT include in your estimate of total hours.

ATTORNEY #1:

     NAME   _____

     FIRM   _____

     ADDRESS _____

     CITY   _____

     STATE   _____ZIP _____

ATTORNEY #2:

     NAME   _____

     FIRM   _____

     ADDRESS _____

     CITY   _____

     STATE   _____ZIP _____

68

22. (CONT.) Please print the names and addresses of attorneys you can NOT include in your estimate of total hours.

ATTORNEY #3:

        NAME   _____

        FIRM   _____

        ADDRESS _____

        CITY   _____

        STATE   _____ ZIP _____

ATTORNEY #4:

        NAME   _____

        FIRM   _____

        ADDRESS _____

        CITY   _____

        STATE   _____ ZIP _____

23. Not counting time spent by those attorneys named in Question 22, what is the approximate TOTAL number of hours worked by you and all other attorneys for your client's side on this dispute? (Do not include time spent in court or appellate litigation.)

        TOTAL ATTORNEY HOURS _____

24. How many of the total number of hours reported in Q.23 were spent on each of the activities listed below? Again do not include activity related to court or appellate litigation.

TOTAL
ATTORNEY HOURS

a   Preparing for filing and all work
    BEFORE administrative proceeding filed. .... _____

b. Hearing time, including time to
    prepare for hearing. .... _____

c. Mediation time, including time to
    prepare for mediation. .... _____

d. Discovery after filing, including
    time related to motions. .... _____

e. Motion practice, excluding discovery. .... _____

d. Any additional time worked AFTER
    filing administrative proceeding, directly
    related to this dispute. .... _____

25. How much were the attorney fees associated with this dispute? Please include fees for all attorneys included in questions 23 and 24. Remember, your best estimate is fine.

TOTAL FEES $_____.00

26. In addition to attorney fees, how much in costs such as travel, research, and any other costs (including staff time, expert witnesses, investigators, etc.) associated with this dispute were incurred? Remember, your best estimate is fine. (If no additional costs were incurred, please enter 0.)

OTHER COSTS $_____.00

27. Did any salaried or pre-paid lawyers such as government lawyers, private lawyers who were salaried employees, or prepaid legal plan lawyers work for your client's side of this dispute?

    (CHECK ONE)

    ☐ 1 Yes
    ☐ 2 No ⇒ Skip to Question 31, Next page

28. What was the approximate TOTAL number of hours that all government lawyers, private lawyers who were salaried employees, or prepaid legal plan lawyers worked on this case?

TOTAL SALARIED OR
PRE-PAID LAWYER HOURS _____

70

29. Please break down the total number of hours worked by pre-paid or salaried lawyers into each of the salary categories listed below. Again, your best estimate will do.

YEARLY SALARY	NUMBER OF HOURS
Less than $50,000	_____
$50,000 - $75,000	_____
$76,000 - $100,000	_____
$101,000 - $125,000	_____
More than $125,000	_____

30   For these government, other salaried, or prepaid legal plan lawyers please estimate all NON-SALARY expenses such as any non-salary staff or experts, investigations, filing fees, transcript fees, copying expenses, and exhibit costs that were paid (or will be paid) by your client(s).

TOTAL EXPENSES FOR
SALARIED/PRE-PAID LAWYERS $_____.00

31. Please estimate any other legal fees and expenses (not reported above) your client(s) paid (or will pay). Remember, your best estimate will do. If there are not additional costs, please enter 0.

TOTAL LEGAL
FEES AND EXPENSES $_____.00

THANK YOU FOR YOUR ASSISTANCE. PLEASE PLACE THIS FORM IN THE ENVELOPE PROVIDED AND (INSERT AGENCY SPECIFIC INSTRUCTIONS HERE).

E. Mediator/Hearing Officer Survey

Introduction

This survey is designed to gather data regarding the mediator's and/or hearing officer's satisfaction with the ADR program rules and procedures and the costs associated with the mediator and/or hearing officer. This survey should be completed by both the mediator and/or the hearing officer assigned to hear the dispute, depending on the procedures applied to the dispute. If the program being evaluated is not a mediation, this survey should be modified to reflect the appropriate characteristics of that program.

Mediator/Hearing Officer Survey

Instructions:

- <u>If you acted as a hearing officer or administrative judge in this dispute, please begin this questionnaire at SECTION B, page 3.</u>

- <u>If you acted as a mediator in this dispute, please begin this questionnaire at SECTION A.</u>

- Please answer each question by checking the appropriate box or filling in a number.

- Skip questions only if you are instructed to do so.

- Please be assured that the information you provide will be kept strictly confidential.

- When you have completed this questionnaire, please place it in the envelope provided and (INSERT AGENCY SPECIFIC INSTRUCTIONS).

Thank you for your assistance.

A. Evaluation Of Mediation (to be completed by Mediators only)

1. Are you familiar with any case selection criteria (AGENCY) uses for mediation?

   ☐ 1 Yes
   ☐ 2 No ⇒ <u>Skip to Question 3</u>

2. Do you believe the case selection criteria are appropriate?

   (CHECK ONE)

   ☐ 1 Yes
   ☐ 2 No

3. Are you aware of any (AGENCY) procedures that provide disputants with information about mediation?

   ☐ 1 Yes
   ☐ 2 No ⇒ <u>Skip to Question 5, Next Page</u>

4. Do you believe the procedures for providing disputants with information are satisfactory?

   (CHECK ONE)

   ☐ 1 Yes
   ☐ 2 No

5. Are you aware of any training (AGENCY) gives disputants to prepare for mediation?

   ☐ 1 Yes
   ☐ 2 No ⇒ <u>Skip to Question 7</u>

6. Do you believe the training to prepare disputants for mediation is satisfactory?

   (CHECK ONE)

   ☐ 1 Yes
   ☐ 2 No

7. In your opinion, what effect did mediation have on time to resolution in this dispute?

   (CHECK ONE)

   ☐ 1 Increased time to resolution
   ☐ 2 No effect
   ☐ 3 Decreased time to resolution
   ☐ 4 Don't know

8. In your opinion, what effect did mediation have on administrative dispute costs for the parties in this dispute?

   (CHECK ONE)

   ☐ 1 Increased dispute costs
   ☐ 2 No effect
   ☐ 3 Decreased dispute costs
   ☐ 4 Don't know

74

9. Was the timing of the mediation appropriate for it to positively contribute to the resolution of this dispute, or would the mediation have been more productive if it were held earlier or later in the process?

    (CHECK ONE)

    ☐ 1 Should have mediated earlier

    ☐ 2 Right time

    ☐ 3 Should have mediated later

    ☐ 4 Dispute not appropriate for mediation

> PLEASE SKIP TO QUESTION 16, PAGE 5.

B. Administrative Judge Evaluation (to be completed by Hearing Officers and Administrative Judges only)

10. Was this dispute mediated through (AGENCY)'s ADR Program?

    (CHECK ONE)

    ☐ 1 Yes ⇒ <u>Skip to Question 13, Next Page</u>

    ☐ 2 No

    ☐ 3 Don't Know ⇒ <u>Skip to Question 16, Page 5</u>

11. If mediation <u>had</u> been used in this dispute, do you think that it would have helped to resolve it in less time?

    (CHECK ONE)

    ☐ 1 Yes

    ☐ 2 No

    ☐ 3 Don't Know

12. If mediation __had__ been used in this dispute, do you think that it would have saved the disputants resources (e.g. staff time and other costs)?

(CHECK ONE)

☐ 1 Yes
☐ 2 No
☐ 3 Don't Know

SKIP TO QUESTION 16, PAGE 5.

13. What do you think of the decision to use mediation in this dispute?

(CHECK ONE)

☐ 1 Mediation was appropriate
☐ 2 Case should __not__ have been mediated

14. In your opinion, what effect did mediation have on time to resolution in this dispute?

(CHECK ONE)

☐ 1 Increased time to resolution
☐ 2 No effect
☐ 3 Decreased time to resolution
☐ 4 Don't know

15. In your opinion, what effect did mediation have on administrative dispute costs for the parties in this dispute?

(CHECK ONE)

☐ 1 Increased dispute costs
☐ 2 No effect
☐ 3 Decreased dispute costs
☐ 4 Don't know

C. Administrative Costs

In order to understand the economic costs of disputes, we need as much information as possible about costs associated with this dispute. We realize records and other information related to your time and costs may not be available. In answering these items, please give us your best estimate of the actual number.

16. Approximately how many hours did you spend on the following:

<u>TOTAL HOURS</u>

    a   Preparing for hearing _____ _____

    b.   Hearing time _____ _____

    c.   Posthearing/Deliberation _____ _____

    d.   Any additional time _____ _____

17. Please check the government pay grade or hourly bill rate that best describes you:

GOVERNMENT EMPLOYEES:
(CHECK ONE)

(INSERT PAY GRADE LIST HERE)

EVERYONE ELSE:
(CHECK ONE)

☐ 1 Under $100

☐ 2 $101-$200

☐ 2 $201-$300

☐ 4 Over $300

18. Who compensates you for your time related to this dispute?

(CHECK ONE)

☐ 1 This agency alone (either through salary or other arrangement)

☐ 2 Disputants together

☐ 3 Some other agency (including your employer)

☐ 4 Other

19. Approximately how much staff costs (such as secretarial, administrative, and any other personnel) were incurred by you or your office related to this dispute? Remember, your best estimate is fine. (If no staff costs were incurred, please enter 0.)

GOVERNMENT EMPLOYEES:

(INSERT HOURS BY PAY GRADE LIST HERE)

EVERYONE ELSE:

WAGE OF STAFF	TOTAL HOURS ALL STAFF AT THIS WAGE
Less than $10 an hour	_____
$10 - $20 an hour	_____
$20 - $40 an hour	_____
$40- $60 an hour	_____
$60 - $80 an hour	_____
$80 - $100 an hour	_____
More than $100 an hour	_____

20. Approximately how much in costs such as travel, research, and any other costs (excluding staff time) associated with this dispute were incurred by you or your office? Remember, your best estimate is fine. (If no additional costs were incurred, please enter 0.)

OTHER COSTS $_____.00

```
THANK YOU FOR YOUR ASSISTANCE. PLEASE PLACE THIS
FORM IN THE ENVELOPE PROVIDED AND (INSERT AGENCY
SPECIFIC INSTRUCTIONS HERE).
```

Bibliography

Adler, J., D. Hensler, and C. Nelson, *Simple Justice: How Litigants Fare in the Pittsburgh Court Arbitration Program*, Santa Monica, Calif.: RAND, R-3071-ICJ, 1983.

Administrative Conference of the United States, *Federal Administrative Procedure Sourcebook*, Washington, D.C.: Office of the Chairman, 1992.

Administrative Conference of the United States, *Federal Agency Use of Alternative Means of Dispute Resolution*, Washington, D.C.: Office of the Chairman, 1987.

Administrative Conference of the United States Dispute, Systems Design Working Group, Evaluation Subgroup, *Performance Indicators for ADR Program Evaluation*, Washington, D.C.: Office of the Chairman, 1993.

Fitz-Gibbon, C., and L. Morris, *How to Design a Program Evaluation*, Newbury Park, Calif.: Sage Publications, Inc., 1987.

Fowler, F., *Survey Research Methods*, Beverly Hills, Calif.: Sage Publications, Inc., 1984.

Herman, J., L. Morris, and C. Fitz-Gibbon, *Evaluator's Handbook*, Newbury Park, Calif.: Sage Publications, Inc., 1987.

Kalton, G., *Introduction to Survey Sampling*, Beverly Hills, Calif.: Sage Publications, Inc., 1983.

Kimmel, Allan J., *Ethics and Values in Applied Social Research*, Beverly Hills, Calif.: Sage Publications, Inc., 1989.

Krueger, R., *Focus Groups: A Practical Guide for Applied Research*, Newbury Park, Calif.: Sage Publications, Inc., 1988.

Lind, E. A., *Arbitrating High Stakes Cases: An Evaluation of Court-Annexed Arbitration in a United States District Court*, Santa Monica, Calif.: RAND, R-3809-ICJ, 1990.

Lind, E. A., R. MacCoun, P. Ebener, W. Felstiner, D. Hensler, J. Resnik, and T. Tyler, *The Perceptions of Justice: Tort Litigants' View of Trial, Court-Annexed Arbitration, and Judicial Settlement Conferences*, Santa Monica, Calif.: RAND, R-3708-ICJ, 1989.

MacCoun, R., E. A. Lind, D. Hensler, D. Bryant, and P. Ebener, *Alternative Adjudication: An Evaluation of the New Jersey Automobile Arbitration Program*, Santa Monica, Calif.: RAND, R-3676-ICJ, 1988.

Patton, M., *How to Use Qualitative Methods in Evaluation*, Newbury Park, Calif.: Sage Publications, Inc., 1987.

Plapinger, E., and M. Shaw, *Court ADR: Elements of Program Design*, New York: Center for Public Resources, 1992.

Rolph, E., *Introducing Court-Annexed Arbitration: A Policymaker's Guide*, Santa Monica, Calif.: RAND, R-3167-ICJ, 1984.

Rossi, P., H. Freeman, and S. Wright, *Evaluation: A Systemic Approach*, Beverly Hills, Calif.: Sage Publications, Inc., 1979.

Stecher, B., and W. A. Davis, *How to Focus an Evaluation*, Newbury Park, Calif.: Sage Publications, Inc., 1987.

ICJ Publications

Outcomes

General

Carroll, S. J., with N. M. Pace, *Assessing the Effects of Tort Reforms*, R-3554-ICJ, 1987.

Galanter, M., B. Garth, D. Hensler, and F. K. Zemans, *How to Improve Civil Justice Policy*, RP-282. (Reprinted from *Judicature*, Vol. 77, No. 4, January/February 1994.)

Hensler, D. R., *Trends in California Tort Liability Litigation*, P-7287-ICJ, 1987. (Testimony before the Select Committee on Insurance, California State Assembly, October 1987.)

_____ , *Researching Civil Justice: Problems and Pitfalls*, P-7604-ICJ, 1988. (Reprinted from *Law and Contemporary Problems*, Vol. 51, No. 3, Summer 1988.)

_____ , *Reading the Tort Litigation Tea Leaves: What's Going on in the Civil Liability System?* RP-226. (Reprinted from *The Justice System Journal*, Vol. 16, No. 2, 1993.)

Hensler, D. R., M. E. Vaiana, J. S. Kakalik, and M. A. Peterson, *Trends in Tort Litigation: The Story Behind the Statistics*, R-3583-ICJ, 1987.

Hill, P. T., and D. L. Madey, *Educational Policymaking Through the Civil Justice System*, R-2904-ICJ, 1982.

Lipson, A. J., *California Enacts Prejudgment Interest: A Case Study of Legislative Action*, N-2096-ICJ, 1984.

Shubert, G. H., *Some Observations on the Need for Tort Reform*, P-7189-ICJ, 1986. (Testimony before the National Conference of State Legislatures, January 1986.)

_____ , *Changes in the Tort System: Helping Inform the Policy Debate*, P-7241-ICJ, 1986.

Jury Verdicts

Carroll, S. J., *Jury Awards and Prejudgment Interest in Tort Cases*, N-1994-ICJ, 1983.

Chin, A., and M. A. Peterson, *Deep Pockets, Empty Pockets: Who Wins in Cook County Jury Trials*, R-3249-ICJ, 1985.

Dertouzos, J. N., E. Holland, and P. A. Ebener, *The Legal and Economic Consequences of Wrongful Termination*, R-3602-ICJ, 1988.

82

Hensler, D. R., *Summary of Research Results on the Tort Liability System*, P-7210-ICJ, 1986. (Testimony before the Committee on Commerce, Science, and Transportation, United States Senate, February 1986.)

MacCoun, R. J., *Getting Inside the Black Box: Toward a Better Understanding of Civil Jury Behavior*, N-2671-ICJ, 1987.

_____ , *Experimental Research on Jury Decisionmaking*, R-3832-ICJ, 1989. (Reprinted from *Science*, Vol. 244, June 1989.)

_____ , *Inside the Black Box: What Empirical Research Tells Us About Decisionmaking by Civil Juries*, RP-238, 1993. (Reprinted from Robert E. Litan, ed., *Verdict: Assessing the Civil Jury System*, The Brookings Institution, 1993.)

_____ , *Is There a "Deep-Pocket" Bias in the Tort System?* IP-130, October 1993.

_____ , *Blaming Others to a Fault?* RP-286. (Reprinted from *Chance*, Vol. 6, No. 4, Fall 1993.)

Peterson, M. A., *Compensation of Injuries: Civil Jury Verdicts in Cook County*, R-3011-ICJ, 1984.

_____ , *Punitive Damages: Preliminary Empirical Findings*, N-2342-ICJ, 1985.

_____ , *Summary of Research Results: Trends and Patterns in Civil Jury Verdicts*, P-7222-ICJ, 1986. (Testimony before the Subcommittee on Oversight, Committee on Ways and Means, United States House of Representatives, March 1986.)

_____ , *Civil Juries in the 1980s: Trends in Jury Trials and Verdicts in California and Cook County, Illinois*, R-3466-ICJ, 1987.

Peterson, M. A., and G. L. Priest, *The Civil Jury: Trends in Trials and Verdicts, Cook County, Illinois, 1960–1979*, R-2881-ICJ, 1982.

Peterson, M. A., S. Sarma, and M. G. Shanley, *Punitive Damages: Empirical Findings*, R-3311-ICJ, 1987.

Selvin, M., and L. Picus, *The Debate over Jury Performance: Observations from a Recent Asbestos Case*, R-3479-ICJ, 1987.

Shanley, M. G., and M. A. Peterson, *Comparative Justice: Civil Jury Verdicts in San Francisco and Cook Counties, 1959–1980*, R-3006-ICJ, 1983.

_____ , *Posttrial Adjustments to Jury Awards*, R-3511-ICJ, 1987.

Costs of Dispute Resolution

Hensler, D. R., *Does ADR Really Save Money? The Jury's Still Out*, RP-327, 1994. (Reprinted from *The National Law Journal*, April 11, 1994.)

Hensler, D. R., M. E. Vaiana, J. S. Kakalik, and M. A. Peterson, *Trends in Tort Litigation: The Story Behind the Statistics*, R-3583-ICJ, 1987.

Kakalik, J. S., and A. E. Robyn, *Costs of the Civil Justice System: Court Expenditures for Processing Tort Cases*, R-2888-ICJ, 1982.

Kakalik, J. S., and R. L. Ross, *Costs of the Civil Justice System: Court Expenditures for Various Types of Civil Cases*, R-2985-ICJ, 1983.

Kakalik, J. S., P. A. Ebener, W. L. F. Felstiner, and M. G. Shanley, *Costs of Asbestos Litigation*, R-3042-ICJ, 1983.

Kakalik, J. S., P. A. Ebener, W. L. F. Felstiner, G. W. Haggstrom, and M. G. Shanley, *Variation in Asbestos Litigation Compensation and Expenses*, R-3132-ICJ, 1984.

Kakalik, J. S., and N. M. Pace, *Costs and Compensation Paid in Tort Litigation*, R-3391-ICJ, 1986.

_____ , *Costs and Compensation Paid in Tort Litigation*, P-7243-ICJ, 1986. (Testimony before the Subcommittee on Trade, Productivity, and Economic Growth, Joint Economic Committee of the Congress, July 1986.)

Kakalik, J. S., E. M. King, M. Traynor, P. A. Ebener, and L. Picus, *Costs and Compensation Paid in Aviation Accident Litigation*, R-3421-ICJ, 1988.

Kakalik, J. S., M. Selvin, and N. M. Pace, *Averting Gridlock: Strategies for Reducing Civil Delay in the Los Angeles Superior Court*, R-3762-ICJ, 1990.

Lind, E. A., *Arbitrating High-Stakes Cases: An Evaluation of Court-Annexed Arbitration in a United States District Court*, R-3809-ICJ, 1990.

MacCoun, R. J., E. A. Lind, D. R. Hensler, D. L. Bryant, and P. A. Ebener, *Alternative Adjudication: An Evaluation of the New Jersey Automobile Arbitration Program*, R-3676-ICJ, 1988.

Peterson, M. A., *New Tools for Reducing Civil Litigation Expenses*, R-3013-ICJ, 1983.

Priest, G. L., *Regulating the Content and Volume of Litigation: An Economic Analysis*, R-3084-ICJ, 1983.

Dispute Resolution

Court Delay

Adler, J. W., W. L. F. Felstiner, D. R. Hensler, and M. A. Peterson, *The Pace of Litigation: Conference Proceedings*, R-2922-ICJ, 1982.

Dungworth, T., and N. M. Pace, *Statistical Overview of Civil Litigation in the Federal Courts*, R-3885-ICJ, 1990.

Ebener, P. A., *Court Efforts to Reduce Pretrial Delay: A National Inventory*, R-2732-ICJ, 1981.

Kakalik, J. S., M. Selvin, and N. M. Pace, *Averting Gridlock: Strategies for Reducing Civil Delay in the Los Angeles Superior Court*, R-3762-ICJ, 1990.

_____ , *Strategies for Reducing Civil Delay in the Los Angeles Superior Court: Technical Appendixes*, N-2988-ICJ, 1990.

Lind, E. A., *Arbitrating High-Stakes Cases: An Evaluation of Court-Annexed Arbitration in a United States District Court*, R-3809-ICJ, 1990.

MacCoun, R. J., E. A. Lind, D. R. Hensler, D. L. Bryant, and P. A. Ebener, *Alternative Adjudication: An Evaluation of the New Jersey Automobile Arbitration Program*, R-3676-ICJ, 1988.

Resnik, J., *Managerial Judges*, R-3002-ICJ, 1982. (Reprinted from the *Harvard Law Review*, Vol. 96:374, December 1982.)

Selvin, M., and P. A. Ebener, *Managing the Unmanageable: A History of Civil Delay in the Los Angeles Superior Court*, R-3165-ICJ, 1984.

Alternative Dispute Resolution

Adler, J. W., D. R. Hensler, and C. E. Nelson, with the assistance of G. J. Rest, *Simple Justice: How Litigants Fare in the Pittsburgh Court Arbitration Program*, R-3071-ICJ, 1983.

Bryant, D. L., *Judicial Arbitration in California: An Update*, N-2909-ICJ, 1989.

Ebener, P. A., and D. R. Betancourt, *Court-Annexed Arbitration: The National Picture*, N-2257-ICJ, 1985.

Hensler, D. R., *Court-Annexed Arbitration in the State Trial Court System*, P-6963-ICJ, 1984. (Testimony before the Judiciary Committee Subcommittee on Courts, United States Senate, February 1984.)

_____ , *Reforming the Civil Litigation Process: How Court Arbitration Can Help*, P-7027-ICJ, 1984. (Reprinted from the *New Jersey Bell Journal*, August 1984.)

_____ , *What We Know and Don't Know About Court-Administered Arbitration*, N-2444-ICJ, 1986.

_____ , *Court-Ordered Arbitration: An Alternative View*, RP-103, 1992. (Reprinted from *The University of Chicago Legal Forum*, Vol. 1990.)

_____ , *Science in the Court: Is There a Role for Alternative Dispute Resolution?* RP-109, 1992. (Reprinted from *Law and Contemporary Problems*, Vol. 54, No. 3, Summer 1991.)

_____ , *Does ADR Really Save Money? The Jury's Still Out*, RP-327, 1994. (Reprinted from *The National Law Journal*, April 11, 1994.)

Hensler, D. R., A. J. Lipson, and E. S. Rolph, *Judicial Arbitration in California: The First Year*, R-2733-ICJ, 1981.

_____ , *Judicial Arbitration in California: The First Year: Executive Summary*, R-2733/1-ICJ, 1981.

Hensler, D. R., and J. W. Adler, with the assistance of G. J. Rest, *Court-Administered Arbitration: An Alternative for Consumer Dispute Resolution*, N-1965-ICJ, 1983.

Lind, E. A., *Arbitrating High-Stakes Cases: An Evaluation of Court-Annexed Arbitration in a United States District Court*, R-3809-ICJ, 1990.

Lind, E. A., R. J. MacCoun, P. A. Ebener, W. L. F. Felstiner, D. R. Hensler, J. Resnik, and T. R. Tyler, *The Perception of Justice: Tort Litigants' Views of Trial, Court-Annexed Arbitration, and Judicial Settlement Conferences*, R-3708-ICJ, 1989.

MacCoun, R. J., *Unintended Consequences of Court Arbitration: A Cautionary Tale from New Jersey*, RP-134, 1992. (Reprinted from *The Justice System Journal*, Vol. 14, No. 2, 1991.)

MacCoun, R. J., E. A. Lind, D. R. Hensler, D. L. Bryant, and P. A. Ebener, *Alternative Adjudication: An Evaluation of the New Jersey Automobile Arbitration Program*, R-3676-ICJ, 1988.

MacCoun, R. J., E. A. Lind, and T. R. Tyler, *Alternative Dispute Resolution in Trial and Appellate Courts*, RP-117, 1992. (Reprinted from *Handbook of Psychology and Law*, 1992.)

Moller, E., E. Rolph, P. Ebener, *Private Dispute Resolution in the Banking Industry*, MR-259-ICJ, 1993.

Rolph, E. S., *Introducing Court-Annexed Arbitration: A Policymaker's Guide*, R-3167-ICJ, 1984.

Rolph, E. S., and D. R. Hensler, *Court-Ordered Arbitration: The California Experience*, N-2186-ICJ, 1984.

Rolph, E. S., E. Moller, and L. Petersen, *Escaping the Courthouse: Private Alternative Dispute Resolution in Los Angeles*, MR-472-JRHD/ICJ, 1994.

Special Issues

Kritzer, H. M., W. L. F. Felstiner, A. Sarat, and D. M. Trubek, *The Impact of Fee Arrangement on Lawyer Effort*, P-7180-ICJ, 1986.

Priest, G. L., *Regulating the Content and Volume of Litigation: An Economic Analysis*, R-3084-ICJ, 1983.

Priest, G. L., and B. Klein, *The Selection of Disputes for Litigation*, R-3032-ICJ, 1984.

Resnik, J., *Managerial Judges*, R-3002-ICJ, 1982. (Reprinted from the *Harvard Law Review*, Vol. 96:374, December 1982.)

_____ , *Failing Faith: Adjudicatory Procedure in Decline*, P-7272-ICJ, 1987. (Reprinted from the *University of Chicago Law Review*, Vol. 53, No. 2, 1986.)

_____ , *Due Process: A Public Dimension*, P-7418-ICJ, 1988. (Reprinted from the *University of Florida Law Review*, Vol. 39, No. 2, 1987.)

_____ , *Judging Consent*, P-7419-ICJ, 1988. (Reprinted from the *University of Chicago Legal Forum*, Vol. 1987.)

_____ , *From "Cases" to "Litigation,"* RP-110, 1992. (Reprinted from *Law and Contemporary Problems*, Vol. 54, No. 3, Summer 1991.)

Areas of Liability

Auto-Accident Litigation

Carroll, S. J., J. S. Kakalik, *No-Fault Approaches to Compensating Auto Accident Victims*, RP-229, 1993. (Reprinted from *The Journal of Risk and Insurance*, Vol. 60, No. 2, 1993.)

Carroll, S. J., J. S. Kakalik, N. M. Pace, and J. L. Adams, *No-Fault Approaches to Compensating People Injured in Automobile Accidents*, R-4019-ICJ, 1991.

Carroll, S. J., J. S. Kakalik, with D. Adamson, *No-Fault Automobile Insurance: A Policy Perspective*, R-4019/1-ICJ, 1991.

Hammitt, J. K., *Automobile Accident Compensation, Volume II, Payments by Auto Insurers*, R-3051-ICJ, 1985.

Hammitt, J. K., and J. E. Rolph, *Limiting Liability for Automobile Accidents: Are No-Fault Tort Thresholds Effective?* N-2418-ICJ, 1985.

Hammitt, J. K., R. L. Houchens, S. S. Polin, and J. E. Rolph, *Automobile Accident Compensation: Volume IV, State Rules*, R-3053-ICJ, 1985.

Houchens, R. L., *Automobile Accident Compensation: Volume III, Payments from All Sources*, R-3052-ICJ, 1985.

MacCoun, R. J., E. A. Lind, D. R. Hensler, D. L. Bryant, and P. A. Ebener, *Alternative Adjudication: An Evaluation of the New Jersey Automobile Arbitration Program*, R-3676-ICJ, 1988.

O'Connell, J., S. J. Carroll, M. Horowitz, and A. Abrahamse, *Consumer Choice in the Auto Insurance Market*, RP-254, 1994. (Reprinted from the *Maryland Law Review*, Vol. 52, 1993.)

Rolph, J. E., with J. K. Hammitt, R. L. Houchens, and S. S. Polin, *Automobile Accident Compensation: Volume I, Who Pays How Much How Soon?* R-3050-ICJ, 1985.

Asbestos

Hensler, D. R., *Resolving Mass Toxic Torts: Myths and Realities*, P-7631-ICJ, 1990. (Reprinted from the *University of Illinois Law Review*, Vol. 1989, No. 1.)

_____ , *Assessing Claims Resolution Facilities: What We Need to Know*, RP-107, 1992. (Reprinted from *Law and Contemporary Problems*, Vol. 53, No. 4, Autumn 1990.)

_____ , *Fashioning a National Resolution of Asbestos Personal Injury Litigation: A Reply to Professor Brickman*, RP-114, 1992. (Reprinted from *Cardozo Law Review*, Vol. 13, No. 6, April 1992.)

Hensler, D. R., W. L. F. Felstiner, M. Selvin, and P. A. Ebener, *Asbestos in the Courts: The Challenge of Mass Toxic Torts*, R-3324-ICJ, 1985.

Kakalik, J. S., P. A. Ebener, W. L. F. Felstiner, and M. G. Shanley, *Costs of Asbestos Litigation*, R-3042-ICJ, 1983.

Kakalik, J. S., P. A. Ebener, W. L. F. Felstiner, G. W. Haggstrom, and M. G. Shanley, *Variation in Asbestos Litigation Compensation and Expenses*, R-3132-ICJ, 1984.

Peterson, M. A., *Giving Away Money: Comparative Comments on Claims Resolution Facilities*, RP-108, 1992. (Reprinted from *Law and Contemporary Problems*, Vol. 53, No. 4, Autumn 1990.)

Peterson, M. A., and M. Selvin, *Resolution of Mass Torts: Toward a Framework for Evaluation of Aggregative Procedures*, N-2805-ICJ, 1988.

_____ , *Mass Justice: The Limited and Unlimited Power of Courts*, RP-116, 1992. (Reprinted from *Law and Contemporary Problems*, No. 3, Summer 1991.)

Selvin, M., and L. Picus, *The Debate over Jury Performance: Observations from a Recent Asbestos Case*, R-3479-ICJ, 1987.

Aviation Accidents

Kakalik, J. S., E. M. King, M. Traynor, P. A. Ebener, and L. Picus, *Costs and Compensation Paid in Aviation Accident Litigation*, R-3421-ICJ, 1988.

_____ , *Aviation Accident Litigation Survey: Data Collection Forms*, N-2773-ICJ, 1988.

King, E. M., and J. P. Smith, *Computing Economic Loss in Cases of Wrongful Death*, R-3549-ICJ, 1988.

_____ , *Economic Loss and Compensation in Aviation Accidents*, R-3551-ICJ, 1988.

_____ , *Dispute Resolution Following Airplane Crashes*, R-3585-ICJ, 1988.

Executive Summaries of the Aviation Accident Study, R-3684, 1988.

Employment

Dertouzos, J. N., E. Holland, and P. A. Ebener, *The Legal and Economic Consequences of Wrongful Termination*, R-3602-ICJ, 1988.

Dertouzos, J. N., and L. A. Karoly, *Labor-Market Responses to Employer Liability*, R-3989-ICJ, 1992.

Environmental Litigation: Superfund

Acton, J. P., *Understanding Superfund: A Progress Report*, R-3838-ICJ, 1989.

Acton, J. P., and L. Dixon with D. Drezner, L. Hill, and S. McKenney, *Superfund and Transaction Costs: The Experiences of Insurers and Very Large Industrial Firms*, R-4132-ICJ, 1992.

Dixon, L., *RAND Research on Superfund Transaction Costs: A Summary of Findings to Date*, CT-111, November 1993.

Dixon, L. S., *Fixing Superfund: The Effect of the Proposed Superfund Reform Act of 1994 on Transaction Costs*, MR-455-ICJ, 1994.

Dixon, L. S., D. S. Drezner, and J. K. Hammitt, *Private-Sector Cleanup Expenditures and Transaction Costs at 18 Superfund Sites*, MR-204-EPA/RC, 1993.

Medical Malpractice

Danzon, P. M., *Contingent Fees for Personal Injury Litigation*, R-2458-HCFA, 1980.

_____ , *The Disposition of Medical Malpractice Claims*, R-2622-HCFA, 1980.

_____ , *Why Are Malpractice Premiums So High—Or So Low?* R-2623-HCFA, 1980.

_____ , *The Frequency and Severity of Medical Malpractice Claims*, R-2870-ICJ/HCFA, 1982.

_____ , *New Evidence on the Frequency and Severity of Medical Malpractice Claims*, R-3410-ICJ, 1986.

_____ , *The Effects of Tort Reform on the Frequency and Severity of Medical Malpractice Claims: A Summary of Research Results*, P-7211, 1986. (Testimony before the Committee on the Judiciary, United States Senate, March 1986.)

Danzon, P. M., and L. A. Lillard, *The Resolution of Medical Malpractice Claims: Modeling the Bargaining Process*, R-2792-ICJ, 1982.

_____ , *Settlement Out of Court: The Disposition of Medical Malpractice Claims*, P-6800, 1982.

_____ , *The Resolution of Medical Malpractice Claims: Research Results and Policy Implications*, R-2793-ICJ, 1982.

Kravitz, R. L. , J. E. Rolph, K. A. McGuigan, *Malpractice Claims Data as a Quality Improvement Tool: I. Epidemiology of Error in Four Specialties*, N-3448/1-RWJ, 1991.

Lewis, E., and J. E. Rolph, *The Bad Apples? Malpractice Claims Experience of Physicians with a Surplus Lines Insurer*, P-7812, 1993.

Rolph, E., *Health Care Delivery and Tort: Systems on a Collision Course?* Conference Proceedings, Dallas, June 1991, N-3524-ICJ, 1992.

Rolph, J. E., *Some Statistical Evidence on Merit Rating in Medical Malpractice Insurance*, N-1725-HHS, 1981.

_____ , *Merit Rating for Physicians' Malpractice Premiums: Only a Modest Deterrent*, N-3426-MT/RWJ/RC, 1991.

Rolph, J. E., R. L. Kravitz, K. A. McGuigan, *Malpractice Claims Data as a Quality Improvement Tool: II. Is Targeting Effective?* N-3448/2-RWJ, 1991.

Williams, A. P., *Malpractice, Outcomes, and Appropriateness of Care*, P-7445, May 1988.

Product Liability

Dungworth, T., *Product Liability and the Business Sector: Litigation Trends in Federal Courts*, R-3668-ICJ, 1988.

Eads, G., and P. Reuter, *Designing Safer Products: Corporate Responses to Product Liability Law and Regulation*, R-3022-ICJ, 1983.

_____ , *Designing Safer Products: Corporate Responses to Product Liability Law and Regulation*, P-7089-ICJ, 1985. (Reprinted from the *Journal of Product Liability*, Vol. 7, 1985.)

Garber, S., *Product Liability and the Economics of Pharmaceuticals and Medical Devices*, R-4285-ICJ, 1993.

Hensler, D. R., *Summary of Research Results on Product Liability*, P-7271-ICJ, 1986. (Statement submitted to the Committee on the Judiciary, United States Senate, October 1986.)

_____ , *What We Know and Don't Know About Product Liability*, P-7775-ICJ, 1993. (Statement submitted to the Commerce Committee, United States Senate, September 1991.)

Peterson, M. A., *Civil Juries in the 1980s: Trends in Jury Trials and Verdicts in California and Cook County, Illinois*, R-3466-ICJ, 1987.

Reuter, P., *The Economic Consequences of Expanded Corporate Liability: An Exploratory Study*, N-2807-ICJ, 1988.

Workers' Compensation

Darling-Hammond, L., and T. J. Kniesner, *The Law and Economics of Workers' Compensation*, R-2716-ICJ, 1980.

Victor, R. B., *Workers' Compensation and Workplace Safety: The Nature of Employer Financial Incentives*, R-2979-ICJ, 1982.

Victor, R. B., L. R. Cohen, and C. E. Phelps, *Workers' Compensation and Workplace Safety: Some Lessons from Economic Theory*, R-2918-ICJ, 1982.

Trends in the Tort Litigation System

Galanter, M., B. Garth, D. Hensler, and F. K. Zemans, *How to Improve Civil Justice Policy*, RP-282. (Reprinted from *Judicature*, Vol. 77, No. 4, January/February 1994.

Hensler, D. R., *Trends in California Tort Liability Litigation*, P-7287-ICJ, 1987. (Testimony before the Select Committee on Insurance, California State Assembly, October 1987.)

_____ , *Reading the Tort Litigation Tea Leaves: What's Going on in the Civil Liability System?* RP-226. (Reprinted from *The Justice System Journal*, Vol. 16, No. 2, 1993.)

Hensler, D. R., M. E. Vaiana, J. S. Kakalik, and M. A. Peterson, *Trends in Tort Litigation: The Story Behind the Statistics*, R-3583-ICJ, 1987.

Mass Torts and Environmental Liability

Mass Torts

Hensler, D. R., *Resolving Mass Toxic Torts: Myths and Realities*, P-7631-ICJ, 1990. (Reprinted from the *University of Illinois Law Review*, Vol. 1989, No. 1.)

_____ , *Asbestos Litigation in the United States: A Brief Overview*, P-7776-ICJ, 1992. (Testimony before the Courts and Judicial Administration Subcommittee, United States House Judiciary Committee, October 1991.)

_____ , *Assessing Claims Resolution Facilities: What We Need to Know*, RP-107, 1992. (Reprinted from *Law and Contemporary Problems*, Vol. 53, No. 4, Autumn 1990.)

_____ , *Fashioning a National Resolution of Asbestos Personal Injury Litigation: A Reply to Professor Brickman*, RP-114, 1992. (Reprinted from *Cardozo Law Review*, Vol. 13, No. 6, April 1992.)

Hensler, D. R., W. L. F. Felstiner, M. Selvin, and P. A. Ebener, *Asbestos in the Courts: The Challenge of Mass Toxic Torts*, R-3324-ICJ, 1985.

Hensler, D. R., M. A. Peterson, *Understanding Mass Personal Injury Litigation: A Socio-Legal Analysis*, RP-311, 1994. (Reprinted from *Brooklyn Law Review*, Vol. 59, No. 3, Fall 1993.)

Kakalik, J. S., P. A. Ebener, W. L. F. Felstiner, G. W. Haggstrom, and M. G. Shanley, *Variation in Asbestos Litigation Compensation and Expenses*, R-3132-ICJ, 1984.

Kakalik, J. S., P. A. Ebener, W. L. F. Felstiner, and M. G. Shanley, *Costs of Asbestos Litigation*, R-3042-ICJ, 1983.

Peterson, M. A., *Giving Away Money: Comparative Comments on Claims Resolution Facilities*, RP-108, 1992. (Reprinted from *Law and Contemporary Problems*, Vol. 53, No. 4, Autumn 1990.)

Peterson, M. A., and M. Selvin, *Resolution of Mass Torts: Toward a Framework for Evaluation of Aggregative Procedures*, N-2805-ICJ, 1988.

_____ , *Mass Justice: The Limited and Unlimited Power of Courts*, RP-116, 1992. (Reprinted from *Law and Contemporary Problems*, Vol. 54, No. 3, Summer 1991.)

Selvin, M., and L. Picus, *The Debate over Jury Performance: Observations from a Recent Asbestos Case*, R-3479-ICJ, 1987.

Environmental Liability: Superfund

Acton, J. P., *Understanding Superfund: A Progress Report*, R-3838-ICJ, 1989.

Acton, J. P., and L. Dixon with D. Drezner, L. Hill, and S. McKenney, *Superfund and Transaction Costs: The Experiences of Insurers and Very Large Industrial Firms*, R-4132-ICJ, 1992.

Dixon, L. *RAND Research on Superfund Transaction Costs: A Summary of Findings to Date*, CT-111, November 1993.

Dixon, L. S., *Fixing Superfund: The Effect of the Proposed Superfund Reform Act of 1994 on Transaction Costs*, MR-455-ICJ, 1994.

Dixon, L. S., D. S. Drezner, J. K. Hammitt, *Private-Sector Cleanup Expenditures and Transaction Costs at 18 Superfund Sites*, MR-204-EPA/RC, 1993.

Reuter, P., *The Economic Consequences of Expanded Corporate Liability: An Exploratory Study*, N-2807-ICJ, 1988.

Economic Effects of the Liability System

General

Johnson, L. L., *Cost-Benefit Analysis and Voluntary Safety Standards for Consumer Products*, R-2882-ICJ, 1982.

Reuter, P., *The Economic Consequences of Expanded Corporate Liability: An Exploratory Study*, N-2807-ICJ, 1988.

Product Liability

Dungworth, T., *Product Liability and the Business Sector: Litigation Trends in Federal Courts*, R-3668-ICJ, 1988.

Eads, G., and P. Reuter, *Designing Safer Products: Corporate Responses to Product Liability Law and Regulation*, R-3022-ICJ, 1983.

_____ , *Designing Safer Products: Corporate Responses to Product Liability Law and Regulation*, P-7089-ICJ, 1985. (Reprinted from the *Journal of Product Liability*, Vol. 7, 1985.)

Garber, S., *Product Liability and the Economics of Pharmaceuticals and Medical Devices*, R-4285-ICJ, 1993.

Hensler, D. R., *Summary of Research Results on Product Liability*, P-7271-ICJ, 1986. (Statement submitted to the Committee on the Judiciary, United States Senate, October 1986.)

_____ , *What We Know and Don't Know About Product Liability*, P-7775-ICJ, 1993. (Statement submitted to the Commerce Committee, United States Senate, September 1991.)

Peterson, M. A., *Civil Juries in the 1980s: Trends in Jury Trials and Verdicts in California and Cook County, Illinois,* R-3466-ICJ, 1987.

Wrongful Termination

Dertouzos, J. N., E. Holland, and P. A. Ebener, *The Legal and Economic Consequences of Wrongful Termination,* R-3602-ICJ, 1988.

Dertouzos, J. N., and L. A. Karoly, *Labor-Market Responses to Employer Liability,* R-3989-ICJ, 1992.

Compensation Systems

System Design

Darling-Hammond, L., and T. J. Kniesner, *The Law and Economics of Workers' Compensation,* R-2716-ICJ, 1980.

Hammitt, J. K., R. L. Houchens, S. S. Polin, and J. E. Rolph, *Automobile Accident Compensation: Volume IV, State Rules,* R-3053-ICJ, 1985.

Hammitt, J. K., and J. E. Rolph, *Limiting Liability for Automobile Accidents: Are No-Fault Tort Thresholds Effective?* N-2418-ICJ, 1985.

Hensler, D. R., *Resolving Mass Toxic Torts: Myths and Realities,* P-7631-ICJ, 1990. (Reprinted from the *University of Illinois Law Review,* Vol. 1989, No. 1.)

_____ , *Assessing Claims Resolution Facilities: What We Need to Know,* RP-107, 1992. (Reprinted from *Law and Contemporary Problems,* Vol. 53, No. 4, Autumn 1990.)

King, E. M., and J. P. Smith, *Computing Economic Loss in Cases of Wrongful Death,* R-3549-ICJ, 1988.

Peterson, M. A., and M. Selvin, *Resolution of Mass Torts: Toward a Framework for Evaluation of Aggregative Procedures,* N-2805-ICJ, 1988.

Rolph, E. S., *Framing the Compensation Inquiry,* RP-115, 1992. (Reprinted from the *Cardozo Law Review,* Vol. 13, No. 6, April 1992.)

Victor, R. B., *Workers' Compensation and Workplace Safety: The Nature of Employer Financial Incentives,* R-2979-ICJ, 1982.

Victor, R. B., L. R. Cohen, and C. E. Phelps, *Workers' Compensation and Workplace Safety: Some Lessons from Economic Theory,* R-2918-ICJ, 1982.

Performance

Carroll, S. J., and J. S. Kakalik, *No-Fault Approaches to Compensating Auto Accident Victims,* RP-229, 1993. (Reprinted from *The Journal of Risk and Insurance,* Vol. 60, No. 2, 1993.)

Carroll, S. J., J. S. Kakalik, N. M. Pace, and J. L. Adams, *No-Fault Approaches to Compensating People Injured in Automobile Accidents*, R-4019-ICJ, 1991.

Carroll, S. J., J. S. Kakalik, with D. Adamson, *No-Fault Automobile Insurance: A Policy Perspective*, R-4019/1-ICJ, 1991.

Hensler, D. R., M. S. Marquis, A. F. Abrahamse, S. H. Berry, P. A. Ebener, E. G. Lewis, E. A. Lind, R. J. MacCoun, W. G. Manning, J. A. Rogowski, and M. E. Vaiana, *Compensation for Accidental Injuries in the United States*, R-3999-HHS/ICJ, 1991.

_____ , *Compensation for Accidental Injuries in the United States: Executive Summary*, R-3999/1-HHS/ICJ, 1991.

_____ , *Compensation for Accidental Injuries: Research Design and Methods*, N-3230-HHS/ICJ, 1991.

King, E. M., and J. P. Smith, *Economic Loss and Compensation in Aviation Accidents*, R-3551-ICJ, 1988.

O'Connell, J., S. J. Carroll, M. Horowitz, and A. Abrahamse, *Consumer Choice in the Auto Insurance Market*, RP-254, 1994. (Reprinted from the *Maryland Law Review*, Vol. 52, 1993.)

Peterson, M. A., *Giving Away Money: Comparative Comments on Claims Resolution Facilities*, RP-108, 1992. (Reprinted from *Law and Contemporary Problems*, Vol. 53, No. 4, Autumn 1990.)

Peterson, M. A., and M. Selvin, *Mass Justice: The Limited and Unlimited Power of Courts*, RP-116, 1992. (Reprinted from *Law and Contemporary Problems*, Vol. 54, No. 3, Summer 1991.)

Rolph, J. E., with J. K. Hammitt, R. L. Houchens, and S. S. Polin, *Automobile Accident Compensation: Volume I, Who Pays How Much How Soon?* R-3050-ICJ, 1985.

Special Studies

Hensler, D. R., and M. E. Reddy, *California Lawyers View the Future: A Report to the Commission on the Future of the Legal Profession and the State Bar*, MR-528-ICJ, 1994.

A special bibliography (CP-253, 12/94) provides a list of RAND publications in the civil justice area. To request the bibliography or to obtain more information about the Institute for Civil Justice, please write the Institute at this address: The Institute for Civil Justice, RAND, 1700 Main Street, P.O. Box 2138, Santa Monica, California 90407-2138, or call (310) 393-0411, x7803. A profile of the ICJ, abstracts of its publications, and ordering information can also be found on RAND's home page on the World Wide Web at **http://www.rand.org/** and on RAND's gopher server at **info.rand.org**.